# The Ultimate New York Wedding

Everything you need to know about getting married in New York

Michele Lo Manto

The Ultimate Wedding Series Press
Books may be purchased by contacting the author at:

www.theultimatenewyorkwedding.com
www.michelelomanto.com

Publisher: The Ultimate Wedding Series Press
Cover Design: Art of Digital Media, Caitlin Dean
Interior Design: Art of Digital Media,
Creative Consultant: Ed Howard, Lauren Levine
Research Assistant: Camilla Jorst
ISBN: 9780692563861
Library of Congress Number: 2016903173
First Edition, 2016
Printed in USA

*To my husband for bringing out the best in me*

# Table of Contents

## Introduction

This book has two souls and they were both equally important in inspiring me to write it. The first is my deep love for the city in which I was born: as a New Yorker, I feel a pinch of pride every time I cross the Brooklyn Bridge or catch a glimpse of the Empire State Building. Even after all these years, the sheer beauty of the city takes my breath away. My second inspiration is the passion I have for my work: as the Director of Social Events at Edison Ballroom for nearly a decade, I have worked with dozens of couples to help them plan and organize the most important day of their lives. Having a small part in someone else's big dream inspires me to be better at work every day.

When I set out to write The Ultimate New York Wedding over two years ago my goal was to condense the experience of my decade-long career in hospitality into 200 pages of valuable information. I wanted to create a "curated directory" for New York brides, full of useful tips and helpful advice. More importantly, I wanted to write something that was easy to consult, a reference tool for all future brides dreaming to get married in the most vibrant, beautiful city in the world. I researched every type of venue big or small, vetted florists, ranked photographers, and sought out non-traditional alternatives, from organic catering to getting married at the zoo. I have sifted through literally hundreds of businesses serving the wedding industry in the five boroughs, eliminating the ones that didn't qualify as professional and incorporating the good ones into a search-friendly resource section at the end of the book. I am confident that this book will save you time and prevent you from making costly mistakes.

I understand that things change fast, especially in a city like New York. Sharing your experience with us will help future brides have their very own ultimate New York wedding. Feel free to send any comments or feedback to michele@theultimatenewyorkwedding.com and I will be sure to incorporate your suggestions into future editions.

Thank you for buying this book and best of luck to you in planning your fabulous New York wedding. I'm sure it will be everything you've ever dreamed of and more!

Michele Lo Manto

# CHAPTER ONE

## Choosing The Perfect Venue

# 1.

## Choosing The Perfect Venue

New York City is home to some of the most celebrated wedding venues in the country. Part of what makes this city so special is not only the vast choices it has to offer, but also the historical element of these classic venues, many of which have been immortalized through books and movies. From grandeur and professionalism to beauty and culture – New York City has it all. There are countless options to explore, and this chapter highlights only a few of the many great options.*

One of the first decisions to explore is whether to get married in a hotel or a banquet hall. This decision can be a hard one, especially because New York has so many fantastic options in both categories.

### Hotel Weddings

The Plaza, The Pierre, and The Waldorf Astoria are definitely the top 3 candidates if you want to get married in a hotel. Many brides have dreamed of getting married in one of these posh hotels, which are all staples located in the heart of New York City. Let's take a closer look at each of these venues.

### The Plaza

The Plaza Hotel's stunning décor and unparalleled reputation makes it one of the most sought-after wedding venues in Manhattan. Right in the heart of the city on Fifth Avenue Central Park South, The Plaza's location is hard to beat. The hotel has two ballrooms to choose from for your wedding, both of which exude timeless elegance. The Grand Ballroom is the larger of the two, with a capacity of 600 guests for a cocktail reception-style setup and 500 guests for a seated dinner. The Terrace Room is slightly smaller, accommodating 500 guests for cocktail reception-style setup and 370 guests for a seated dinner. For a wedding at The Plaza, expect to pay a hefty room rental fee plus food and beverage costs for the hotel's exclusive in-house catering.

*For a more comprehensive list of venues, refer to the resource section at the end of this book.

## The Pierre

The Pierre ranks consistently among New York City's top wedding venues with its mix of old-world glamour and modern flair. It is located across from Central Park, making it a perfect choice for couples who want to be photographed in New York City's most iconic park. The Pierre has multiple rooms to choose from for your wedding, each with the high level of privacy and exclusivity that is expected. This hotel is a great option for larger weddings, with a maximum capacity of 1,500 for a cocktail reception-style setup and 800 guests for a seated dinner.

## The Waldorf-Astoria

Located on Park Avenue in Midtown Manhattan, The Waldorf-Astoria is one of the most luxurious wedding venues in all of New York City. The Waldorf has multiple options to choose from, each room with its own distinct style and elegant setting. From the Grand Ballroom that is inspired by the Court Theatre in Versailles to the Starlight Roof with its Art Deco grillwork ceiling, this venue is truly one of the most beautiful and sophisticated. The Waldorf can accommodate large weddings, with a maximum capacity of 1,000 guests for a seated dinner.

## Private Venues

New York City has some of the best banquet halls in the nation. Several dedicated venues in Manhattan specialize in weddings, including Cipriani, Edison Ballroom, Capitale, Gotham Hall, and Espace.

## Cipriani

Cipriani's international brand makes it a highly sought-after venue for native New Yorkers and foreigners alike. Cipriani has three different locations in New York City: Cipriani Wall Street, Cipriani 23rd Street (on Fifth Avenue), and Cipriani 42nd Street (near Grand Central Station). With three separate locations throughout Manhattan, Cipriani provides the flexibility that most other venues can't offer. Cipriani's convenience and brand recognition, however, certainly comes at a hefty price tag for its customers.

### The Edison Ballroom

Edison Ballroom is an elegant private event space located in the heart of Times Square. With its long history dating back to 1932, the venue embodies old New York at its finest. This historical venue re-opened in 2008 after a multimillion-dollar renovation that restored it to its original glory. With plush leather walls, illuminated glass tiles, and grand crystal chandeliers, the décor is best described as "art deco flair with a modern twist." The venue has three rooms with a stunning mezzanine that directly overlooks the main ballroom. The Edison Ballroom is the perfect venue choice for a classic, yet stylish New York City wedding.

### Capitale

Capitale, which was formerly the Bowery Savings Bank, is located in a less-than desirable neighborhood near China Town. The building underwent a $1 million-dollar renovation that converted it from a bank into an event space. The building's neoclassical architecture was restored during the renovation, creating a unique backdrop for events. Although the location of the venue is lacking, the beauty of the space certainly makes up for its sub-par location.

### Gotham Hall

Located in Midtown Manhattan, Gotham Hall is another example of a bank that was turned into an event space. Originally constructed in the 1920's as the Greenwich Savings Bank, the building became Gotham Hall at the turn of the century. The venue has a more corporate feel, as the building still retains much of the architecture and décor from when it was a bank. However, these features certainly create a unique atmosphere for a wedding venue.

### Espace

Espace is located in Midtown Manhattan on West 42nd Street. With its mix of all black and white colors, the venue has a modern, yet sophisticated look. Espace's minimalistic décor is perfect for couples who want to bring in their own unique setup for their event. If you're looking for a blank canvas to create the wedding of your dreams, Espace is the perfect match for you.

Edison Ballroom is a classic venue that embodies old New York at its finest.

## Outdoor Venues

What about venues with outdoor options? Outdoor weddings are lovely and certainly make for a memorable experience when the weather is beautiful. However, keep in mind that there is an obvious inherent risk in planning an outdoor wedding. If you are the type of person that needs full control over every aspect of your big day, it may be best to stick with an indoor wedding venue. That being said, Manhattan has a few beautiful options for outdoor weddings.

### Central Park

With its picturesque views and natural setting, Central Park is the quintessential outdoor New York City experience. With many hotels and indoor venues nearby, many couples opt to have their ceremony in Central Park before moving to a separate site for their reception. For those couples who prefer to host their entire wedding outdoors, a picnic reception is a nice compliment to a Central Park ceremony. There are many different locations available within the park depending on your party size. The most popular of these locations include The Pond, Cop Cot, Shakespeare Garden, Ladies Pavilion and Cherry Hill.

Central Park could very well be one of the most beautiful backdrops for your wedding, but there are certain things you'll need to consider before booking your wedding there. There are strict regulations in place to preserve the natural setting of the park; for example, chairs, tents, and certain decorations are prohibited because of the potential damage to the soil. Also, alcohol is not permitted in any New York City park whatsoever. That's right - if you choose Central Park for your wedding reception, there will be no sipping on Champagnes or Cosmopolitans to celebrate your big day. If "No Alcohol" is simply not an option for your wedding, you'll need to move the party outside of the park after your ceremony.

As is the case with any outdoor venue, the beauty of a Central Park wedding is entirely weather-dependent. If any forecast other than clear skies will absolutely ruin your wedding day, keep an open mind about having an indoor wedding. One bride I worked with at Edison Ballroom always dreamed of an autumn wedding in Central Park, but she didn't want to leave anything

Inspired by the beauty of Central Park, this bride completely transformed
the art deco Edison Ballroom into a nature-filled venue.

to chance – especially the weather. So, we brought Central Park to her. To this day, I've never seen such an imaginative venue transformation. It was straight out of a nature-filled fairy tale, and this bride for her special day was an autumn princess indeed!

## Midtown Loft & Terrace

Located on Fifth Avenue in Midtown, Midtown Loft & Terrace has stunning views of the Empire State Building and Manhattan skyline on its 360° wrap-around rooftop terrace. While the roof itself is an independent space equipped with a kitchen, bathrooms, and an enclosed lounge area with a working fireplace, many couples choose to move to the loft below for dinner once their ceremony has ended. The loft has high ceilings and seats 180 guests for dinner. With windows on all four sides of the loft, guests can enjoy the beautiful city views to the fullest.

## Elevated Acre

This acre-sized outdoor area in Lower Manhattan is one of New York City's best-kept secrets. Hidden among the bustling Financial District, Elevated Acre is located 40 feet above ground with beautifully maintained landscaping and a garden full of ornamental plants. With stunning views of Brooklyn Heights, the Brooklyn Bridge, and the Hudson River, guests are sure to have a real downtown New York City experience. Couples can rent a tent and have their entire wedding at Elevated Acre, or they can move around the corner after the ceremony to the nearby India House venue for their reception.

## 620 Rooftop Garden

Located on Fifth Avenue in Midtown, 620 Rooftop Garden is a great option for small weddings with a maximum of 120 guests. This rooftop garden on the 7th floor of Rockefeller Center's British Empire Building showcases views of Saint Patrick's Cathedral and Saks Fifth Avenue. The garden is ideal for the ceremony. After the ceremony, guests can move into the Soho-style interior loft space for the reception.

***

These are just a handful of some of the great wedding venues that New York City has to offer. These locations and many other New York wedding venues can be found in the resource section at the end of this book. With dozens of venues to choose from, you'll definitely find one that is the perfect match for you!

# CHAPTER TWO

## Non-Traditional Wedding Venues

# 2.

# Non-Traditional Wedding Venues

Do you love New York but hate the idea of a traditional hotel or ballroom wedding? If your answer is an emphatic "Yes!", then this section was written especially for you. In this chapter, you'll learn how to incorporate fun New York City themes into your special, slightly offbeat wedding to create an event that your guests will never forget.

## Boat Weddings

One of the most popular ideas for a non-traditional wedding is getting married on a boat. With beautiful views in the sunset, your guests have the opportunity to experience New York City in a very special way. Boat weddings also make for beautiful photo ops that other venues simply can't offer. There are various companies in New York City that offer boat weddings, all with different pick-up and drop-off locations throughout the city.*

Circle Line Sightseeing Cruises is a popular option for Manhattan boat weddings.

*See the resource section at the end of the book for a list of boat companies in New York City that offer wedding services.

Boat weddings come in all different styles and sizes. Are you the adventurous type that loves being out on the water, or an all-too-fabulous bride that is strictly committed to luxury for her big day? Luckily, you can rent anything from sailboats to yachts in New York City. The price for a boat wedding usually includes a flat rate for the rental of the boat, plus an additional amount per guest. You should go over all pricing with boat rental companies that you are considering in great detail.

There are some obvious drawbacks to consider when getting married on a boat. Like any outdoor venue, boat weddings are highly dependent on weather. If the unpredictability of the weather makes you uncomfortable, there are many indoor non-traditional wedding venues that I cover later in this chapter. Also, keep in mind that boats are not for everyone. Some of your guests may not like being in a confined space and others may easily become seasick.

Of course, you are the star of the show at your wedding, but you should still be considerate of guests who are coming to share in your special day. Consult with some of your family and close friends – if you are the only one getting excited by the idea of a boat wedding, it is probably best to pass on the idea. If you absolutely must incorporate a boat into your wedding somehow, then consider using a boat for your engagement party, bridal shower, bachelorette party, or rehearsal dinner.

## The New York Stock Exchange

Do you and your fiancé happen to love finance? If so, the New York Stock Exchange could be the perfect wedding venue for you. The New York Stock Exchange can accommodate both small and large weddings, ranging anywhere from 20 to 500 guests. The Main Dining Room has a maximum capacity of 350 guests for a cocktail reception-style setup and 300 guests for a seated dinner. The Trading Floor can accommodate up to 500 guests for a cocktail reception-style setup.

The New York Stock Exchange represents an important part of New York City culture and it can be a unique setting for a wedding. However, keep in mind that because it is a landmark building, your creative freedom is somewhat limited, especially if you are using the Trading Floor. Aside from this minor drawback, a wedding at the New York Stock Exchange could be a fun idea. After all, what better place is there to get married for two finance lovers in the finance capital of the world?

# Museum Weddings

With their beauty and rich cultural history, museums are the perfect setting for a non-traditional wedding. New York City has many different museums, each providing its own unique experience. While pricing can vary greatly depending on the museum, there are many options available for different budgets. Popular New York City museums for weddings include The New York Public Library, The Metropolitan Museum of Art (The Met), The American Museum of Natural History, The Frick Collection, The New Museum, and The Museum of the City of New York. Let's take a look at some of these locations in greater detail.

## The New York Public Library

New York Public Library is the second largest public library in the United States and the fourth largest in the world. The size, beauty, and history of the Library's landmark Stephen A. Schwarzman Building make it the perfect fit for a unique, yet classic New York City wedding. The Knot voted New York Public Library's Steven A. Schwarzman Building as "Best of Weddings (Venue)" in 2012, 2013 and 2014.

With 7 rooms to choose from, this iconic building has plenty of options for your wedding. Its maximum capacity is 750 guests for a cocktail reception-style setup and 450 guests for a seated dinner. The room rental fee for The New York Public Library includes the use of two rooms. On top of the room rental fee, clients can expect to pay an additional per person fee for food and beverage costs. Weddings held at The New York Public Library are typically 5 hours long, which is standard across many other venues throughout Manhattan.

## The Metropolitan Museum of Art (The Met)

With over two million works of art, The Metropolitan Museum of Art (The Met) is the largest art museum in the United States. Although The Met makes a beautiful backdrop for a wedding, this option is not open to everyone, as you must be a corporate patron to host your wedding there. The Met's maximum capacity is 1,000 guests for a cocktail reception-style setup and 550 guests for a seated dinner.

## The American Museum of Natural History

Located on the Upper West Side, The American Museum of Natural History is one of the largest museums in the world, making it a great venue for larger weddings. For private events, the museum has a maximum capacity of 3,000 guests for a cocktail reception-style setup and 1,000 guests for a seated dinner. With over 9 rooms to choose from, you'll find a setting in The American Museum of Natural History that best suits your style.

Getting married underneath the giant blue whale in the American Museum of Natural History is a special New York City experience.

## The Frick Collection

For medium-sized weddings, the former stately home of Henry Clay Frick is your best option. Now a world-class museum, The Frick Collection has over 3 rooms to choose from for your wedding. Its maximum capacity is 500 guests for a cocktail reception-style setup and 200 guests for a seated dinner. Like most museums, The Frick Collection has a room rental fee and an additional per person fee for food and beverage costs. If your heart is set on a wedding at the beautiful Frick Collection, keep in mind that you'll need to work around the museum's time restrictions, as it only allows weddings during the hours of 7 pm to midnight.

## The New Museum

The New Museum is a great, affordable option for smaller weddings. The museum has two rooms to choose from, with a maximum capacity of 250 guests for a cocktail reception-style setup and 120 guests for a seated dinner. The room rental fee for The New Museum is quite reasonable compared to that of other museums in New York City. However, you must make a contribution to the museum in order to host your wedding there. Time restrictions for The New Museum are somewhat flexible, but you are limited to an 8-hour event.

## Zoo Weddings

If you are an animal lover like me, you may have always dreamed of saying "I Do" at the zoo. With the perfect mix of quirkiness and elegance, zoos are the ultimate one-of-a-kind wedding experience. The ability to get up-close-and-personal with zoo animals provides hours of entertainment for your guests; and while there are many great outdoor options in New York City for your wedding, being immersed in wildlife is a feeling that simply can't be replicated with flowers and trees alone.

With several zoos in Manhattan and the outer boroughs that allow weddings, you have plenty of flexibility in terms of location. You will also be pleased to know that your wedding will help a great cause, as all event proceeds help support the Wildlife Conservation Society's mission to help save wildlife and wild places around the world.

## The Central Park Zoo

For couples looking to get married inside Manhattan, The Central Park Zoo is the best option. The zoo is centrally located, just a few yards away from 5th Avenue between 63rd and 66th streets. With its exotic wildlife, stunning skyline views and elegant architecture, The Central Park Zoo creates an unforgettable backdrop for a New York City wedding. The Central Park Zoo is best for medium-sized weddings, with a maximum capacity of 380 guests for a seated dinner.

## The Bronx Zoo

The Bronx Zoo is one of the largest zoos in the world and its versatility makes it a great option for weddings. Your wedding ceremony can be held outdoors among free roaming Indian Peacocks in the historic Astor Court, or inside the timeless, elegant Beaux-Arts Zoo Center. With two rooms to choose from for your reception, the Bronx Zoo is ideal for both small and medium-sized weddings. The Congo Gorilla Forrest can accommodate up to 80 guests for a seated dinner, and the recently renovated Schiff Family Great Hall can accommodate up to 225 guests for a seated dinner.

There are certain restrictions to consider when planning your wedding at the Bronx Zoo. For example, your wedding must be held between the hours of 6 pm and 11 pm. You must also use the venue's exclusive in-house catering for events.

## The Prospect Park Zoo

For a fun Brooklyn experience, The Prospect Park Zoo is your place. This 12-acre zoo located off Flatbush Avenue has plenty of entertainment for your guests – from the sea lions performing during cocktail hour to hanging out with the wallabies and kangaroos. The Prospect Park Zoo is ideal for smaller weddings, as the venue only accommodates up to 150 guests for a seated dinner.

Special Tip: The NY Aquarium was temporarily closed for private events after the effects of Hurricane Sandy, but it is set to reopen for weddings in late 2016.

## University Chapels

Did you meet your sweetheart on campus in New York City? There are two New York City universities with chapels available for wedding ceremonies – Columbia University and Fordham University. Unfortunately, New York University does not have a chapel that is suitable for weddings at this time.

### Columbia University

On the campus of Columbia University, you can get married in St. Paul's Chapel, a historic landmark of New York City. The chapel can seat up to 400 guests on the main floor and 610 guests when using the upper balconies. About 75 couples marry in St. Paul's Chapel each year and no affiliation with the chapel is required to wed. There are certain restrictions to keep in mind for St. Paul's Chapel. For example, no aisle runners or balloons are allowed inside the chapel. It is also prohibited to throw objects like rice or rose petals, which many couples typically use to celebrate their union.

> Special Tip: For a wedding reception on campus, many couples choose The Faculty House at Columbia University. This versatile, multi-level venue can accommodate up to 250 guests for a seated dinner in its formal banquet hall located on the third level of the building. On the fourth level, guests can enjoy the outdoor terrace that overlooks the beautiful Manhattan skyline.

### Fordham University

The Fordham University Church located on Rose Hill Campus in the Bronx is a Gothic-style church that was built in 1845. While this location is absolutely beautiful, there are various restrictions for holding your wedding ceremony there. The church is only available for sacramental Catholic weddings and you must be a student, staff member, or alumnus of Fordham University to wed on campus. The ceremony must take place on a Saturday or Sunday, and advanced planning with the university is required. The Office of Campus Ministry at Rose Hill is the department at Fordham University that handles marriage arrangements for the university church.

## Skydive Weddings

The sky takes the award for the most eccentric non-traditional wedding venue. With its exhilarating experience and unbeatable birds-eye views, skydiving is the ultimate way for thrill-seeking couples to commit to one another. Jumping out of a plane during your vows takes the typical adrenaline rush of weddings to an entirely new level! You'll even have amazing wedding photos to remember your big day.

As thrilling as skydiving may be, there are some obvious drawbacks of marrying in the sky. There will likely be little to no guests watching you exchange vows; so, if you've always dreamed getting married in front a large group of family and friends, a skydive wedding is not the right fit for you. You will also need to find an officiant who will agree to marry you in the sky, which is a difficult task in itself. Nonetheless, if you are determined to marry in this awesome and original way, you can start your research by checking out the resource section at the end of this book!

***

New York is full of non-traditional wedding options – it what makes New York weddings among the greatest in the world! For a detailed list of all the non-traditional wedding options listed here, refer to the resource section at the end of the book.

# CHAPTER THREE

## Specialty Weddings

# 3.
## Specialty Weddings

New York City is home to hundreds of different ethnic groups – it is part of what makes this city so special. If you are looking to incorporate your cultural traditions into your wedding day, New York City makes it easy for you to do so. With access to Manhattan's various vendors you have the ability to craft an experience for your guests that stays true to your ethnic roots. If you are planning a Jewish, Indian, Russian, or Greek wedding in New York, then this chapter is for you. Here are some tips and ideas to help you plan your cultural wedding in the greatest city in the world.

### Jewish Wedding

A Jewish wedding ceremony follows Jewish law and traditions. Common traditions of a Jewish ceremony include signing of the Ketubah (marriage contract) prior to the ceremony, standing under a chuppah (canopy) during the ceremony, and breaking of the glass by the groom at the end of the ceremony. Jewish weddings are generally prohibited on Shabbat and during Jewish holidays. It is important to keep these restrictions in mind when planning your Jewish wedding.

> Special Tip: Converse sneakers are not suitable for breaking the glass at the end of a Jewish ceremony! One of the grooms that I worked with at Edison Ballroom made the awful mistake of wearing converse sneakers and he badly injured his foot when breaking the glass. Luckily, there was a doctor on-site to attend to his injured foot, so the groom was able to enjoy the rest of his wedding night. However, he did need to go to the hospital the next day to get stitches in his foot.

Many venues in New York City either provide Kosher food or allow outside Kosher caterers provide food for events when required. The Edison Ballroom and Espace are among the many New York City venues that allow outside

Kosher catering for events. If you require a strictly Kosher menu for your wedding, there are a number of reputable Kosher caterers in the New York area. Among these caterers are Foremost RAM Caterers, Prestige Caterers, and Esprit Events. If you are less strict about adhering to Jewish tradition, you may consider having a "Kosher-style" menu. Kosher-style means that all shellfish and pork are omitted from the menu. It also prohibits the mixing of any dairy and meat products. Most banquet halls with in-house catering will offer a Kosher-style menu as an option. However, it is important to understand that Kosher-style menus are not actually Kosher according to traditional Halachic standards. If you are perfectly fine with a Kosher-style menu but have a handful of guests that need Kosher meals, then speak with your venue about ordering Kosher meals for these guests only. Make sure to ask the price for Kosher meals, as the cost will likely be added to your final bill.

In terms of special décor, you will need a chuppah for your Jewish wedding ceremony. A chuppah is a canopy that couples stand under during the ceremony, which symbolizes the home that the couple will build together. Many décor companies should be able to order and decorate your chuppah for you, matching it to your event décor. However, if you plan to order and decorate your own chuppah, a couple of New York-based chuppah rental companies include Your Chuppah NY and Chuppah Rental NYC.

Here is one of the many beautiful chuppah decorations that I've seen at Edison Ballroom.

## Indian Wedding

Did you know that Indian weddings (also called "South Asian weddings") are filled with ritual and ceremony? These weddings often take place over several days, with a strong emphasis placed on family and the union of the newly married couple.

The pre-wedding party and ceremony for Indian weddings are often held outdoors, making parks, yacht clubs, and other outdoor venues particularly popular among Indian couples. Indoor venues also work well for Indian couples, as many New York venues can easily be decorated with traditional South Asian décor. Espace, for example, holds many South Asian weddings because the venue is easily customizable with any décor. The Edison Ballroom has also hosted several stunning, tradition-filled Indian weddings.

There is no shortage of Indian caterers in New York City, and many of them specialize in weddings. The Indian Clove, for example, has great reviews and an expansive menu, and it is often described as "Indian cuisine with an inspired twist." Other popular Indian caterers for weddings include Darbar Catering Services, Devi, and Bukhara Grill.

Event design companies are instrumental in transforming an ordinary venue into a festive South Asian celebration. Some of the top décor companies in the northeast that specialize in South Asian event décor include Elegant Affairs, Evenings of Elegance, and Shagun Design. Some photography companies in the New York area that specialize in Indian weddings and South Asian events include Pandya Photography, Pacific Pictures, and Nayeem Vohra Photography and Cinematography.

## Russian Wedding

Russians sure know how to throw a party! Russian weddings usually last for at least two days, and some even take place over the course of an entire week. Like any other Russian celebration, a Russian wedding includes dancing, singing, long toasts, and plenty of food and drinks. Many venues located just outside of Manhattan are popular among the Russian community for weddings. In Staten Island, for example, are Nicotra's Ballroom and

EDISON BALLROOM

This Indian couple hosted thier festive wedding at Edison Ballroom in 2015.

The Vanderbilt. In Brooklyn, popular venues for Russian weddings include Passages and Orion Palace. An abundance of tasty, traditional food is required for any Russian celebration. If a venue does not specialize in Russian catering, it may allow couples to bring in an outside Russian caterer for their wedding. Some Russian caterers in New York include Mari Vanna Restaurant, Onegin, and Russian Samovar.

There are many companies in the greater New York area that specialize in Russian entertainment. Barynya Entertainment is one of the leading Russian Entertainment companies. It contracts private entertainers for events – providing everything from DJ's and bands to ballet performers and balalaika players. Barynya Entertainment lists all of its entertainers on the company website, so you can look them up online for more information.

## Greek Wedding

Greek Orthodox wedding ceremonies usually take place in a Greek Orthodox Church. There are several Greek Orthodox Churches in New York City, including Annunciation Greek Orthodox Church, Archdiocesan Cathedral of the Holy Trinity, Saint John the Baptist Greek Orthodox Church, Saint George Greek Orthodox Church, and Saint Barbara Greek Orthodox Church. Although all venues in New York City are suitable for hosting Greek weddings, you'll want to ask venues about their policy for incorporating certain Greek traditions into your event. For example, some venues may not allow smashing of plates, which is a traditional Greek folk custom during celebrations.

There are several companies in New York City that specialize in Greek entertainment for weddings. The Apollo Orchestras, which offers different wedding packages, helps match you with the perfect singers and entertainers for your event. Another company, Europa Sounds, specializes in Greek-American music and offers both live music and DJ / MC services. There are also several photographers in the area that specialize in Greek Weddings. GK Photography, which is well-known in the Greek community, documents weddings in a photojournalistic way. Another popular photographer is Christos Hountas, who uses naturally expressive imagery to capture the special moments from your wedding.

\*\*\*

While the vendors listed in this chapter specialize in weddings of a certain culture, most New York vendors have the ability and experience to accommodate any type of specialty wedding. Make sure to check out the resource section at the end of the book for a full list of wedding vendors.

# CHAPTER FOUR

## Catering

# 4.

## Catering

Great food is the secret to making your guests happy. This is especially true in New York – a city full of self-proclaimed foodies with high expectations. Beyond impressing your guests with delicious food, your wedding menu gives you an opportunity to personalize your event. Are you and your fiancé constantly seeking out the hottest new restaurants? Or are you die-hard comfort food fans? Whichever style you opt for, selecting your wedding menu is an important task that will set the tone for the entire party. Therefore, it's wise to spend some time thinking about your menu and the type of dining experience you'd like to create for your guests.

Raw Bar station from the Edison Ballroom menu.

In this chapter, I discuss the difference between in-house and outside catering for venues. I also cover some of the best event caterers in New York City, broken down by category. If you appreciate food as much as I do, get ready for a great read!

## In-house vs. Outside Catering

Some venues provide in-house catering for events. While some of these venues may allow you to use an outside caterer for your wedding, many require that you use their in-house catering in order to host your event there. This means that if you absolutely fall in love with a wedding venue that provides in-house catering, but you already have a caterer in mind that you'd like to use, you may ultimately need to choose between the two. One of the first questions you should ask early in your venue search is whether the venue provides in-house catering and if so, if use of an outside caterer is permitted.

There are certain cases when a venue with required in-house catering will make an exception to the rule. For example, if you are using a caterer for cultural or religious purposes, then you may be able to bypass the required in-house catering policy and hire an outside caterer. At Edison Ballroom and Espace, we normally require that clients use our in-house catering, but we do make exceptions for Kosher caterers and caterers that specialize in certain cultural or ethnic cuisines. Each venue has different policies for which caterers they allow on-site, so it's important to ask venues about this early on in the planning process.

Most venues with required in-house catering allow you to schedule a tasting once the event is booked. Tastings are important for planning the menu and flow of food, so you should take advantage of any tastings that are offered. Tastings also give you an opportunity to try all of the great food that you'll be too busy to eat on your wedding day!

If your wedding venue does not have in-house catering available, or if it allows you to use an outside caterer for your event, then you will need to start your search for a caterer. Here are some well-known New York City caterers to consider.*

*All the caterers mentioned here and many other great New York caterers are included in the resource section at the back of the book.

## Classic Caterers

### Abigail Kirsch

Abigail Kirsch is one of the leading caterers in New York and the tri-state area. With over 30 years of experience in the industry, the company is known for its high standard of culinary excellence and innovation. Favorite dishes include BLT shortcake bites, foie gras doughnuts and deconstructed banana splits.

### Elegant Affairs

Elegant Affairs caterer is a favorite among celebrities and chic Hamptons socialites. While its food is best described as "American cuisine with a serious kick," the Culinary Team can also customize a menu for your themed event. Some of its inventive dishes include Potato-Crusted Tilapia Provencale and Roasted-beet Lotus Cups with Fig Scented Boursin.

### Peter Callahan

Peter Callahan Catering is a culinary design studio focused on producing experiential events and never-before-seen products. The catering team brings innovative ideas to life, turning savory dishes and sweet bites into imaginative conversation pieces. Its versatile offerings include everything from gourmet feasts to his special take on Pigs and Blankets and Grilled Cheese Sandwiches.

### Creative Edge Parties

For over 25 years, Creative Edge Parties has tailored menus to fit each couples' tastes. Believing that each wedding should reflect the Bride and Groom's individual personalities, it executes events with a high standard of culinary excellence. Offerings include Burrata Caprese Crostini and Grass-fed Filet Mignon.

### Robbins Wolfe Eventeurs

The Robbins Wolfe Eventeurs chefs are versatile pros that specialize in classic dishes with an upscale twist. The company caters to a high-end clientele and has an unparalleled reputation for outstanding professionalism. Signature dishes include Surf and Turf and Grilled Marinated Montauk Striped Bass.

## Sterling Affairs

Sterling Affairs is a high-end catering company with more than 25 years of experience. Its food is best described as New American with French, Mediterranean, and Latin influences. The Sterling Affairs chefs create seasonal menus driven by locally sourced products. In addition to New American dishes, they can also cater elaborate ethnic wedding feasts upon request. Seasonal Spring Entrées include Miso Glazed Cod and Mint Dusted All Natural Colorado Lamb.

## Thomas Preti Events to Savor

For over 25 years, Thomas Preti Events to Savor has provided clients with innovative culinary design. Thomas Preti, the owner and creative force behind this top catering company, is known as a "jack-of-all-trades" when it comes to food. His signature menu offerings include tasting plates and dessert samplers.

## Union Square Events

Union Square Events offers creative, seasonal menus from the chefs at Blue Smoke, Gramercy Tavern and other restaurants of Union Square Hospitality Group. CEO and culinary impresario Danny Meyer has used his vast hospitality experience to help Union Square Events emerge as a leader in its industry. For its seasonal menus, chefs source ingredients from local farmers, artisans and suppliers.

## Eco-Friendly/Organic Caterers

## The Cleaver Co.

The Cleaver Co. is one of the top green caterers of New York, known for its emphasis on high-quality, local ingredients and longstanding commitment to sustainable fishing and humane livestock practices. The Cleaver Co. chefs consider catering as performance art, working together with clients to create a personalized menu. Signature dishes for a summer wedding include Roasted Wild Striped Bass, Grilled Herbed Pork Chops, and Blue Corn Empanadas.

### Catering by Restaurant Associates

Catering by Restaurant Associates is one of the premiere caterers of New York at the forefront of sustainability and social and environmental responsibility. Its professional catering staff and customizable menu featuring seasonal, local ingredients make it a favorite among its high-end clientele.

### Cloud Catering

Cloud Catering's mission is to make every event a celebration. It visits local farms and greenmarkets to get the freshest fish, meat and organic produce for its menu. Signature spring entrees include Bacon Wrapped Pork Loin, Slow-Roasted Short Rib, and Arctic Char.

### Cobblestone Catering

Cobblestone Catering is one of New York's finest boutique caterers that places an emphasis on fresh and local ingredients. Although its menu is drawn from New American cuisine, its chefs will work with clients to customize their menu. The Farm to Table Spring Wedding Menu includes hors d'oeuvres like Tiny Lobster Club, B.L.T. Bites, and Mini Lamb Tamales.

### Great Performances

Great Performances caters everything from intimate gatherings to large elaborate events. It sources produce, meat, fish, and diary from local growers and purveyors to offer clients the best ingredients of the season. Great Performances tailors menus to each event, offering innovative and delicious dishes with only the best ingredients.

### Le Moulin Event Planning & Catering

Over the past 20 years, Le Moulin has earned a reputation for its fine cuisine, impeccable service, and attention to detail. Fresh, local ingredients are the staple of all Le Moulin's menus. Its Seasonal Spring menu includes dishes like Portuguese Crab Cake, Pan Roasted Tournedos of Beef, and Roasted Leg of Lamb.

## Miss Elisabeth's Catering

Executive Chef Elisabeth Weinberg is the star behind Miss Elizabeth's Catering. Weinberg graduated from the French Culinary Institute and later went on to become a Food Network "Chopped!" champion. She uses local, seasonal, and organic ingredients when designing custom menus with her clients. The Elegant Summer Sit Down Dinner Menu includes dishes like Pan Seared Local Sea Scallops, Homemade White Corn Ravioli, and Basil Crusted Lamb Loin.

> Fun Fact: Like Chef Elisabeth Weinberg of Miss Elisabeth's Catering, our very own Edison Ballroom Executive Chef Mina Newman is also a Food Network "Chopped!" Champion.

## Themed Menus

Are you considering a fun themed menu for your wedding? If so, then take a look at some of the caterers listed below. All of these catering companies offer thier own themed menus, which are sure to leave an impression on your guests.

## Blue Smoke Catering

Inspired by the evolving American South, Blue Smoke Catering offers a soulful selection of smoked meats, fresh produce, and thoughtfully sourced ingredients. Blue Smoke Catering delivers the same quality experience that you've come to expect in its restaurant. Chef Kenny Callaghan's Old Hickory pits smoke everything from Pulled Pork to Memphis-Style Baby Back Ribs.

## Fig and Pig Catering

Fig and Pig Catering specializes in comfort finger foods with a high-end twist. It uses seasonal ingredients and a highly professional execution of technique for its comforting, yet contemporary menu. Fig and Pig's sample wedding menu includes hors d'oeuvres like Pulled Pork Sliders with Spicy Pickle, Mini Lobster Roll, and Baby Red Potato stuffed with Chorizo, Chives, and Vermont Cheddar.

## Mary Guiliani Catering & Events

Mary Guiliani Catering and Events puts a chic twist on comfort foods. It brings a creative, customizable approach to high-end catering, drawing inspiration from New York City's fashion, arts and entertainment communities. Signature items include treats like Truffle and Foie Gras Grilled Cheese Sandwiches and Spicy Parmesan Tartlets.

## Pies-N-Thighs

Pies-N-Thighs' comfort foods are inspired by classic American dishes, Mexican and Californian cuisine, and the Slow Food movement's attention to ingredients. The sample wedding menu includes items like Fried Chicken, BBQ Brisket, and Mac & Cheese Biscuits Cornbread.

## The Raging Skillet

The Raging Skillet is best known for its anti-caterer feel and wild, off-the-wall style. It prides itself on being the go-to caterer for non-traditional weddings and events. The Raging Skillet's food reflects fusions from Korea, Thailand, Cuba, Morocco, Jamaica, and more – making it the perfect caterer choice for multicultural weddings.

## Sips & Bites

Sips & Bites specializes in modern versions of comfort food. It believes in creating honest, simple food, using organic and local ingredients whenever possible. Its Summer Wedding Menu includes hors d'oeuvres like Mini Chicken and Waffles, Mini 5-Spice Pulled Pork Sliders, and Goat Cheese & Fig Crostini.

## Tom Orlando Events

Tom Orlando Events has been providing unique catering services to New York and locations all over the world for over 20 years. It offers themed menus that combine elegance and comfort to create a memorable experience. Its Formal Menu includes dishes like Herb Crusted Rack of Lamb served with Potato Pie with Black Truffle Oil. The specialty Backyard BBQ Menu features items like Barbecue Baby Back Ribs, Five Colored Potato Salad, and Watermelon Jicama Salad.

## Oysters XO New York

Oysters XO New York is a raw bar catering company that delivers an innovative culinary experience to party guests. Its Oyster Girls and Oyster Guys walk among the crowd, shucking and serving tasty, high-quality oysters. Oysters XO New York is the perfect way to spice up your cocktail hour in a unique, totally unexpected way.

## Customizable Menus

Customizable menus are a fun way to personalize and brand your event. At Edison Ballroom, we provide clients with an opportunity to personalize their menu as a form of creative expression. Our award-winning Executive Chef Mina Newman can work with clients to create dishes that match the culinary roots of their heritage. She has even recreated special family recipes that have been passed down for generations. Pictured on the following page are a few customizable menu options and food presentations that Executive Chef Mina Newman created for past Edison Ballroom clients. In fact, the dishes were such a hit that we incorporated them into our regular menu after the event!

The use of customizable menus to create a distinct culinary experience is definitely a growing trend in the events industry. Here are a couple other New York caterers that specialize in creating customizable menus for their clients.

## FCI Catering and Events

FCI Catering and Events is known for its fresh, creative innovations. This boutique caterer gets its name from its world-renowned parent company, the International Culinary Center, founded as the French Culinary Institute. FCI marries client customization with culinary inspiration to create everything from classic to contemporary experiences.

## Red Table Catering

Red Table Catering is a Brooklyn-based catering company specializing in hearty, home-cooked food. It offers custom-designed, seasonal menus using only the freshest ingredients from the city's finest butchers, farmers' markets and specialty shops. Red Table Catering will collaborate with couples to include their favorite dishes and family recipes on the menu.

Executive Chef Mina Newman created these Japanese-inspired Italian Pastas for a Japanese-Italian wedding at Edison Ballroom.

Executive Chef Mina Newman created these Mini Meat Crockpots for a French wedding at Edison Ballroom.

***

The caterers listed in this chapter are only a few of the endless caterering options available to you in New York.  Be sure to check out the resource section at the end of the book for a more comprehensive list of caterers in the New York area that specialize in weddings.

# CHAPTER FIVE

## Bridal Necessities

# 5.

# Bridal Necessities

Every bride has dreamed of her wedding day for as long as she can remember. She's envisioned exactly what she will look like walking down that aisle, sometimes before a groom is even in the picture! Perhaps you've always known the style wedding gown that you've wanted; or maybe only now are you beginning to realize the overwhelming number of choices for your wedding day attire. Regardless of what stage you are at in the wedding planning process, this chapter is meant to help you find the best bridal attire and accessories – from your bridal gown to those fabulous headpieces for your flower girls.*

## Wedding Gown

Oh, the wedding gown! It's usually the most important thing on a bride's mind as her wedding day approaches. All eyes are on her as she walks down that aisle, and her future husband will remember how she looks in this moment for many years to come. Needless to say, that bridal gown better look good! Here are some of the best bridal salons in New York City that you can visit to find your perfect dress.

### Kleinfeld Bridal

Kleinfeld Bridal has the largest selection of wedding gowns in the world from American and European designers. With nearly 200 experienced, professional stylists and bridal consultants on-site, Kleinfeld's sells more gowns than any store on earth.

### Pronovias

Located in Midtown on East 52nd Street, Pronovias has a large selection of stunning designer gowns and spacious dressing rooms. Founded in Barcelona, Spain, Pronovias brings a European flair to the American bridal market.

*Check out the resource section at the end of the book for a full list of bridal necessities and vendors.

The salon works by appointment only, so you must schedule an appointment in advance.  In addition to its beautiful selection of gowns, Pronovias also carries a wide variety of jewelry and accessories.

## Bergdorf Goodman Bridal Salon

The Bergdorf Goodman Bridal Salon on Fifth Avenue has an unparalleled selection of exquisite wedding gowns.  Bergdorf provides brides with expert recommendations and offers a comprehensive suite of premiere services for the entire wedding party.  Some of the featured collections at Bergdorf Goodman Bridal Salon include Carolina Herrera, Oscar De La Renta, Monique Lhuillier, and Marchesa.

## Saks Fifth Avenue Bridal Boutique

The Saks Fifth Avenue Bridal Boutique was The Knot's "Best of Weddings" pick in 2009. This bridal boutique offers dresses from a variety of designers and sells veils, headpieces and accessories. Alteration experts are available in-store.  The Saks Fifth Avenue Bridal Boutique can also give you recommendations for cleaning and preservation specialists.

## Designer Loft Bridal

Designer Loft Bridal features today's top and emerging bridal couture designers, some of whom are exclusively featured at Designer Loft Bridal. The bridal shop features non-traditional wedding gowns organized into sections by type (i.e. lace, sparkle, etc.), and provides an easy and comfortable experience for the bride and her wedding party. Alterations are available in-house.

## Saja Wedding

Saja Wedding is a tiny, by appointment-only bridal salon featuring unique, goddess-looking dresses that you won't find anywhere else. Designer Yoo Lee is also the owner of the store, so you get to enjoy on-the-spot styling advice as you shop. Most dresses are reasonably priced, making it the perfect salon for brides on a budget.

### Bridal Reflections

In its newly expanded Fifth Avenue salon, Bridal Reflections offers a variety of dresses from the foremost designers in bridal wear. Family owned and operated for over 40 years, Bridal Reflections is committed to quality and believes in providing a comfortable, unhurried experience for its clients. Bridal Reflections was recently voted "most chic" by Brides Magazine. In addition to bridal gowns, the salon carries a full range of veils, headpieces, and other bridal accessories.

> Special Tip: I purchased my wedding gown at Bridal Reflections on Fifth Avenue and had the most wonderful experience there! From the selection of gorgeous gowns to the warm, attentive staff and expert seamstress – I could not have been happier with Bridal Reflections. Everyone there helped make me a very happy bride on the most important day of my life!

### Selia Yang

Wedding dress designer Selia Yang, who is known for her modern and sophisticated dresses, is the back-to-back winner of The Knot's "Best of Weddings, Designers NYC" award. The design house offers two bridal lines: Couture and The Selia Yang Collection. Alterations are not included.

### Gabriella New York

Gabriella New York is a warm, welcoming boutique that specializes in unique dresses, veils, and headpieces that can't be found anywhere else in New York City. Prices range from moderate to high and alterations are not included.

### The Bridal Garden

The Bridal Garden is the only not-for-profit bridal boutique in New York City, featuring donated designer wedding gowns at up to 75% off the original retail price. The Bridal Garden is the perfect choice for philanthropic brides, as proceeds go towards programs benefitting New York City children's education. Alterations are not included in the price.

Here I am in my dream wedding gown, purchased at Bridal Reflections. In case you are
wondering, my gown was designed by Galia Lahav. Bridal Reflections is the exclusive carrier
of the Galia Lahav collections in New York.

## Shoes

Forget diamonds – shoes are the new "girl's best friend!" Shoes are the focus of a woman's wardrobe throughout the year, and her wedding day is no different. Here are some popular shoe designers among brides for their wedding day.

### Christian Louboutin

Christian Louboutin is a well-respected, well-recognized brand in the fashion industry. A bride can't go wrong with a brand new pair of Louboutin's for her big day, but she can expect to drop a pretty penny on these iconic shoes. One popular Louboutin shoe for brides is the 'Livree' satin peep toe pump.

### Jimmy Choo

Brides that wear Jimmy Choo heels on their big day are looking to make a bold statement, but they can expect to pay a premium for this popular name brand. A popular Jimmy Choo heel among brides is the 'Luna' open toe pump.

### BCBG Max Azria

For the budget-conscious bride, BCBG is a great option for bridal shoes. Brides can choose from a wide selection of different colors, fabrics, and styles, including pumps, slingbacks and flats.

### Kathryn Amberleigh

Kathryn Amberleigh specializes in handmade, offbeat shoes to spice up a bride's wedding day look. Some of these fun, unique shoes include sequined metallic platforms and zebra striped peep toe pumps. If you're looking to stand out in your own special way, this is the perfect designer for you.

# Jewelry

No wedding outfit is complete without the proper jewelry. Luckily, when it comes to jewelry, New York is probably the best city in the world to shop!

## Cartier

Cartier has a variety of stunning, timeless collections that are sure to please every bride. Brides can expect to pay a hefty price for Cartier's quality and unparalleled customer service.

## Tiffany & Co.

Tiffany & Co., a premier and trusted jeweler since 1837, features creations of timeless beauty and extraordinary craftsmanship. Brides can expect to pay a premium for Tiffany & Co.'s brand recognition and quality. Tiffany & Co. has three store locations throughout Manhattan.

## Thomas Laine

Thomas Laine specializes in bridal and special occasions jewelry. It features a variety of collections at different price points to fit every bride's needs. Brides can book showroom appointments or schedule consultations by email or phone.

## Regina B. Jewelry

The Regina B. Jewelry showroom carries couture bridal jewelry, head-pieces, sashes, and veils. Appointments can be made to visit the New York showroom, which features a full-range of couture bridal earrings, wedding necklaces, bridal combs, and wedding veils. Custom-made pieces are available upon request.

## Lola & Madison

Lola & Madison specializes in bridal jewelry and wedding accessories. Designer and owner Lola's inspiration comes from the 1920's Hollywood and Art Deco movement, which is expressed in luxurious materials like French lace, silks and crystals. Lola & Madison's line features jewelry, hair adornments, sashes, garters, veils, and brooch bouquets. All pieces are handcrafted in New York City.

### Greenwich Jewelers

Greenwich Jewelers is a downtown New York City designer jewelry boutique that has been family owned since the 1970's. The store has a personally curated collection of jewelry and a trusted, knowledgeable staff. Greenwich Jewelers also offers resizing and refreshing of existing jewelry.

### Elleven

Elleven is a fine jewelry boutique located in Brooklyn, New York. With its mix of designs and vintage pieces, Elleven offers unique and affordable engagement rings, earrings, necklaces, bracelets, cufflinks, and more.

### Norman Landsberg

Norman Landsberg has been New York's trusted choice for designer diamond jewelry and diamond engagement rings since the 1940's. Its experienced staff has a depth of expertise to help ensure that brides have a comfortable, successful experience. Norman Landsberg has been featured in The Knot's "Best of Weddings."

### Salvatore and Co.

Salvatore and Co., located in the heart of New York City's Diamond District, specializes in diamond engagement rings. It offers hands-on-service and has earned its reputation for unsurpassed honesty and integrity. The majority of its jewelry is designed and manufactured in New York City.

> Special Tip: For diamonds and engagement rings, you must visit the Diamond District on 47th Street. You will get the best deal available, as these shops offer wholesale prices instead of retail prices. It is also quite the shopping experience! My husband bought my engagement ring and our wedding rings at Leon Diamond in the Diamond District on 47th Street.

## Veils And Headpieces

### Sposabella Lace

Sposabella Lace crafts beaded headpieces from a variety of elegant fabrics. Known for its quick order turnaround, this shop is the perfect choice for last-minute brides.

### Monvieve

Monvieve is the world's most exclusive haute couture bridal veil and headpiece company. This Italian brand creates luxury veils from Italian-made tulle and Chantilly lace, and its headpieces embody the sophistication and glamour of French couture. Monvieve is considered a high-fashion collection for women, with every item made-to-order and fully produced by hand in Italy. Brides can expect to pay a higher price Monvieve's quality products. Its midtown New York City store works by appointment only.

### M&J Bridal Salon

M&J's exquisite new bridal salon offers a large selection of beautiful headpieces embellished with items like Swarovski crystals and silk flowers. It also has a selection of bridal gloves, jewelry, shoes, and handbags available in-store. M&J Bridal Salon allows brides to completely customize veils from start to finish, choosing the style, cut, color, length, and fabric of their veil.

### Basia Custom Headdresses and Accessories

Basia Custom Headdresses and Accessories offers elegant, understated headpieces embellished with items like ribbons, pearls, feathers, and Swarovski crystals. Basia Custom Headdresses and Accessories works by appointment only and offers low to moderately priced items.

### Ellen Christine Millinery

Ellen Christine Millinery specializes in custom hats and headpieces adorned with handmade flowers and vintage veiling. This West Village store works by appointment only and offers low to moderately priced items.

## Bridesmaid Dresses

Selecting the perfect dresses for your bridesmaids is an important task. Your bridesmaids are a crucial part of your ceremony and wedding photos, so it's wise to spend time thinking about the color, fabric, and look of these dresses. If selected correctly, your bridesmaid dresses can help complement the overall vibe you are trying to create for your wedding. Here are some stores in New York City that specialize in bridesmaid dresses.

### Bella's Bridesmaids

Bella's Bridesmaids is a national chain that carries top designers like Monique Lhuillier and Jenny Yoo. The store, which is located in Midtown on 38th Street, carries dresses that are moderately priced.

### Claudia Hanlin's Wedding Library

Located on East 60th street, Claudia Hanlin's Wedding Library stocks over 200 styles of moderately priced bridesmaids dresses. Claudia Hanlin's Wedding Library is the flagship store for the popular Amsale bridesmaid line.

### Here Comes the Bridesmaid

Here Comes the Bridesmaid carries more than 400 styles of dresses. Its dresses are moderately priced and styles range from familiar to unusual. Here Comes the Bridesmaid, which is located in Midtown on 37th Street, operates by-appointment only.

***

The categories covered in this chapter are only a few of the many details a bride needs to think about when preparing for her wedding day. For a list of additional vendors and bridal necessities, check out the resource section at the back of this book!

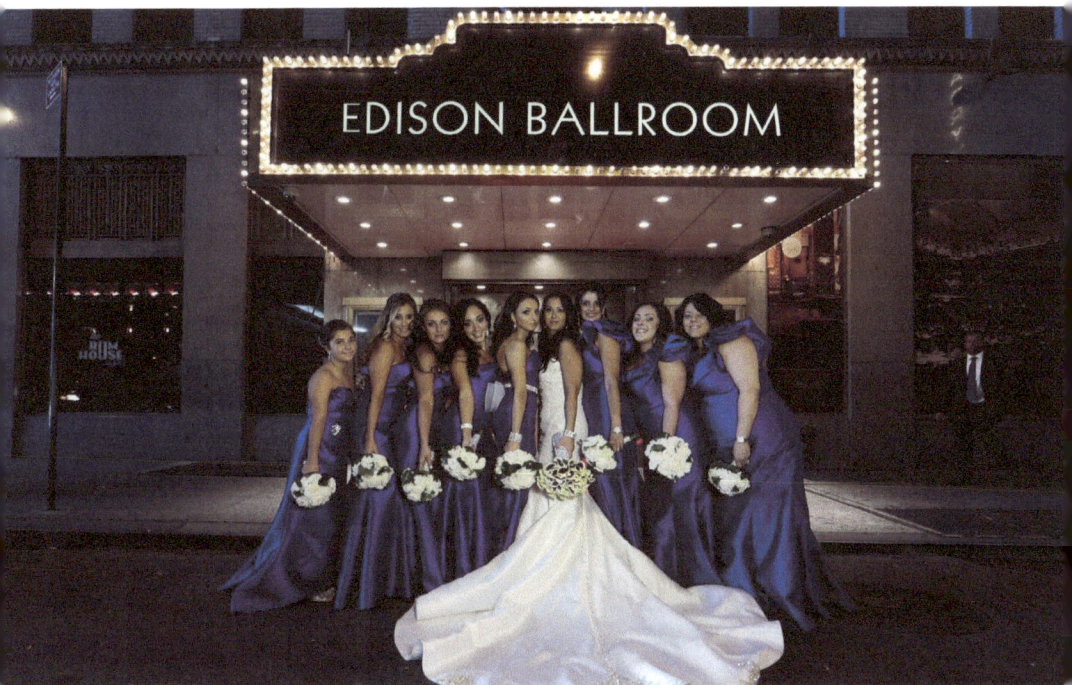

One bride I worked with at Edison Ballroom selected dark purple bridesmaid dresses to match her purple wedding décor.

This Edison Ballroom bride chose bold leopard-print bridesmaid dresses for her quirky, punk rock wedding.

# CHAPTER SIX

## Choosing the Right Wedding Vendors

# 6.

## Choosing the Right Wedding Vendors

I t's finally time to start thinking about all the small details that will come together to make your wedding day unforgettable! This starts, of course, with selecting your wedding vendors. Choosing the right vendors is not an easy task. Between the flowers, cake, photos, and music, there is so much to think about and it is easy to become overwhelmed.

This chapter is meant to help simplify the daunting task of selecting the right wedding vendors. It covers everything from top New York City event planners to the best wedding cake bakers. I even share some personal tips that I've learned over the years to help you make your wedding stand out. Read on to learn more about choosing the right wedding vendors for your big day.

### Event Planners

Sure, you don't need an event planner, but planning a wedding is a lot less stressful with a trusted planner by your side. The money that you spend on a planner is often well worth it because their expertise can help you navigate through the planning process and avoid any unnecessary expenses. The existing relationships that planners have with vendors in the industry also give you access to a network of vetted wedding professionals with a proven track record.

Some brides may feel that that an event planner is unnecessary; they may prefer to plan everything on their own and allocate their wedding budget towards something else that they feel is more important. Other brides may welcome the idea of using an event planner to help ensure that their wedding day runs as smoothly as possible. If you are the latter of the two brides, then this section was written for you! Here are some of the top event planners in the New York City area – many of which I have had the pleasure of working with over the years.

## Gourmet Advisory Services

Gourmet Advisory Services is the nation's premier event planning and party coordination consultancy. Founded by legendary event producer Harriet Rose Katz, Gourmet Advisory provides full-service coordination of design, catering, and event logistics to help you plan your perfect wedding. Katz, who was named "Number One Wedding Planner in Manhattan" by New York Metro, has been quoted as an industry expert in leading wedding publications, such as The New York Times, Modern Bride, New England Bride, and Grace Ormonde's Wedding Style Magazine. At Gourmet Advisory Services, Katz leads a team of talented party planners who have more than a half-century of experience in producing fabulous, one-of-a kind events.

One Edison Ballroom couple learned about this fantastic string ensemble for their ceremony after hiring Gourmet Advisory as their event planner.

## Save the Date

Save the Date has been one of the premiere event planning companies in New York City for over 20 years. Save the Date can help clients with every aspect of their wedding, including venue selection, planning, vendor selection, event production and more. Save the Date differentiates itself from other wedding planners based on its vast industry experience. Unlike other planners who use the same five or six vendors for every event, Save the Date has relationships with thousands of vendors to match each client's needs, expectations, and budget. Save the Date and its Founder Jennifer Gilbert have received numerous awards for their impact on the event planning industry.

## Victoria Dubin Events

Victoria Dubin Events is a full-service event planning and design company. With strong industry connections, endless creative resources, and many years of experience in the event planning industry, Victoria Dubin Events ensures that your wedding will run as smoothly as possible. Dubin's team orchestrates every aspect of the wedding, including venue selection, entertainment, invitations, décor, catering, photography, rentals, party favors, and more. Victoria Dubin Events was recently featured in the Spring/Summer issue of the Grace Ormonde Wedding Style magazine.

## Music

Great music is the key to keeping your guests on the dance floor all night long. The difference between an awesome and average wedding could very well be a result of the music; it can literally make or break your party. Make sure you spend some time thinking about the music for your wedding – your guests will thank you for it!

So, the next question is – "Do I hire a band or a DJ?" Most clients that I work with prefer to hire a band for their wedding. However, there is a trend among younger couples to hire a DJ instead. In my opinion, both live music and DJs are great for weddings – the choice ultimately comes down to your personal preference. Of course, you can opt for the best of both worlds and hire both a band and a DJ. This is a particularly popular option if a couple has allotted time for an after party in their event timeline.

Bands are a favorite among Edison Ballroom wedding clients.

Here are some of the top New York-based production and entertainment companies for weddings. Some of the entertainment companies listed here provide both band and DJ options, while others specialize in only one form of music entertainment.

## Element Music (Band)

Element Music is an exclusive boutique production company founded by Marianne Bennett, a live entertainment producer with over 15 years of experience. Element Music provides a wide range of talent and ensembles comprised of the hottest dancers, choreographers, singers and musicians. Performances include everything from classic ensembles to fifteen-piece bands to match the right feel and tone of your event. Element Music's high-profile clientele include names like Tommy Hilfiger, Ralph Lauren, and Mariah Carey.

Marianne Bennett Orchestra, one of Element Music's most sought after bands, is a must-book for weddings. Bennett and her accomplished players pack bass, drums, and plenty of soul into the evening to impress your guests and keep them wanting more. If you're considering Marianne Bennett Orchestra for your wedding, be sure to schedule ahead, as they book at least nine months in advance.

## Total Entertainment  (Band & DJ)

Total Entertainment is a talented team of event producers with over 20 years of experience. Totally Live!, which is part of the Total Entertainment family, provides premiere live music for weddings.  Its bands are versatile and feature a variety of vocalists who specialize in all genres of music. With its combination of sophistication and fun, Totally Live! and Total Entertainment are favorites among leading venues and wedding planners in New York City and across the nation.

## Hank Lane Music & Productions (Band & DJ)

Hank Lane Music & Productions has dominated the wedding band and music scene for years.  With over 25 years of experience in the industry, Hank Lane has been recognized by many popular wedding publications as one of New York's top choices for wedding dance bands.  Editors of theknot.com named Hank Lane "The Best in New York" after thousands of couples in the New York Metro area voted for the entertainment company.  Hank Lane has also been "Brides Choice" on weddingwire.com since 2010.

Hank Lane has over twenty dance bands that perform a variety of musical styles, including Classic Rock sounds of the 1950's and 1960's, Motown, Disco, 1980's, Hip Hop, and contemporary hits. This company can also provide music for the wedding ceremony. While each of its bands is capable of performing beautiful ceremony music, Hank Lane has an in-house classical department dedicated to providing the finest string ensembles for wedding ceremonies.

To meet the growing demand for DJ entertainment, Hank Lane created More than Music  – a DJ and party entertainment service that offers hot, young DJs with MTV-style dancers and party entertainers.

## Scratch Weddings (DJ)

Scratch Weddings is a wedding DJ service that provides access to the country's leading wedding DJs. The company assigns a dedicated music manager for each event to provide the utmost quality in service to each of its clients. Scratch Weddings has received recognition as the wedding DJ of choice from some of the most trusted wedding publications, including Wedding Wire, The Knot, and Manhattan Bride.  With its insurance policy and host of backup DJs, Scratch Weddings provides a stress-free experience for couples.

**Interview with Hector Velazquez, Creative Director at Total Entertainment**

### How important is music at a wedding?

Music is the most important key to a happy crowd. You can have a venue with great food and mind blowing décor, but without amazing music your guests just leave feeling flat. If you have a combination of a beautiful venue, great food and amazing music, you make memories for a life time!

### I love seeing people of all ages dancing... as a musician, how hard is it to make everyone happy?

Captivating a crowd of both young and old is always a challenge. Having a broad knowledge of music and the ability to read the crowd's reactions on a continual basis is the key to composing your music properly.

## What is the all-time most requested song?

Yikes... I would have to say it's a tie between Sweet Caroline (Neil Diamond) and Don't Stop Believing (Journey)

### What do you think works best for weddings – a band or DJ? Why?

Having the right band for your wedding is the way to go. The energy that the band members project through the music can rock a crowd. Again, the key word is the RIGHT band. I do personally feel that going the route of a band DJ combo is the way the go, at the end of the day you get the best of both worlds.

### I think Edison Ballroom is one of the most "music-friendly" venues in New York, why do you think the room works so well for live music / entertainment?

The layout, acoustics, and stage of Edison Ballroom are conducive to live music. This, along with the supper club look and feel of the Edison Ballroom only adds to the mood that helps energize the guests.

# Photography

You've worked tirelessly for months (maybe even years) to plan the perfect wedding – then in one night, it's all over. Of course, you'll have memories of your wedding fixed forever in your mind, but your wedding photos are the real way that you'll remember your special day for many years to come.

I suggest spending ample time with your photographer to explain the feeling that you want to capture through your photos. Are formal family shots the most important thing to you? Or would you rather document the entire wedding in a more natural, photojournalistic style? Perhaps you'd like to remember your wedding day through editorial style portraits and photos. Whatever your preference is – it's important that you think about these questions early on in the planning process. Understanding your own preference in photography styles will help you select the right wedding photographer for your big day.

Here are some incredibly talented photographers in the New York area that I have had the pleasure of working with over the years at Edison Ballroom.

## Matthew Sowa Photography

Matthew Sowa is a photographer based in downtown New York who specializes in contemporary photography. His photographs have appeared in well-known magazines and have been widely acclaimed at various exhibits. Matthew has received several awards from top wedding publications, including "The Knot Best of Weddings," "Wedding Wire Bride's Choice Awards," and "Wedding Wire Couples' Choice Award." Matthew's creativity and beautiful shots have consistently yielded him exceptional reviews from his past clients.

Special Tip: I used Matthew Sowa for my wedding and he was truly a creative genius! I have been in the wedding industry for nearly a decade and have worked with many top wedding photographers, but my husband and I were really looking for something edgy and different for our wedding. My husband took the lead on finding our wedding photographer and I have to say, Matthew Sowa was the best find of all my wedding vendors!

Here I am in Matthew Sowa's pre-wedding shots at the W Hotel Bridal Suite.

Matthew Sowa took portrait shots of us in Times Square before the ceremony.

## Fred Marcus Studio

In business since 1941, Fred Marcus Studio has built a reputation for quality that has brought many high-end clients in the New York area through its door. The father-and-son duo Andy and Brian Marcus and their associates specialize in both classic portrait and candid photography. Fred Marcus Studio has photographed the weddings of clients like Eddie Murphy, Donald Trump, Kelsey Grammer, and Mary Tyler Moore.

## Brian Dorsey Studios

Brian Dorsey is one of the most sought after photographers in the wedding industry. American Photo named Brian Dorsey one of the world's top 10 wedding photographers, and Dorsey's associate Ron Antonelli recently received the same honor. Dorsey is a regular contributor to New York Magazine, Town & Country, Style Me Pretty, and The Knot. His work often appears in popular publications like The New York Times, Martha Stewart Weddings, and many international publications.

Brian Dorsey captured this Edison Ballroom couple's First Look in Times Square before the ceremony.

## Interview with Brian Dorsey, Founder/Principal Photographer at Brian Dorsey Studios

**You are responsible for making the bride look gorgeous for many years after the wedding date. I feel that pictures are so important in a wedding, are you ever nervous?**

I feel that we're taking the most important pictures in a person's entire life. So there's a lot of pressure. I do get nervous - even after shooting over 200 weddings - not nervous about doing a great job - I'm nervous because I feel obligated to blow everybody away with my photographs every single time in situations where I have very little control. It's the pressure that I put on myself that I feel.

**New York is an amazing city, tell us about your favorite locations to photograph**

I love using the streets as a backdrop. There's so much going on - the energy of the city comes through the photograph. It's also the best background to define where we are in time - a park will always looks like a park - but in 20 years the spots that we shoot in the city will look very different than they do today.

**Color or Black and White?**

Yes. I love rich and vibrant photographs but I also believe that if the color isn't adding to the photograph then it's probably detracting from it.

**I know how hard it is to take good pictures on a packed dance floor... your shots are always beautiful, what is your secret?**

Shooting the action of a party well is another skill set entirely. It's about participating, watching and predicting. You have to be feeling the vibe and the music and then you have to know when and where that split second that differentiates looking crazy and looking great will occur.

**How far in advance do you suggest brides book their photographers?**

Couples should book their photographer and band as soon as they book their venue. Those who create the cakes and florals will always take on another client. When a photographer or a band gets booked that's it – they're no longer an option for you so you shouldn't wait at all on those two.

## Jurick Photography

Over the past decade, Michael Jurick has been recognized as one of the top family photographers in New York City. He is also a favorite among professionals in the event planning industry. Michael is a preferred photography vendor for many top New York City venues, such as The Ritz-Carlton, Westchester, Guastavino's, and Three Sixty°. Jurick has won many awards throughout his career, including the 2010 Julie B. Style Awards in Best of Arts Photography, Nickelodeon Best Family Photographer Award, and the 2012 Red Tricycle Totally Awesome Photographer Award for the New York Metro Area. Jurick is a contributing photographer to Getty Images and has contributed photographs to the New York Times, Rolling Stone, and numerous Conde Nast publications.

## Hechler Photographers

Hechler Photographers, a family business that has been passed down from father to son, includes a team of talented photographers that strive for storytelling perfection. Lead photographer David Hechler and the entire Hechler team capture every emotion in the most natural, unobtrusive way. While Hechler Photographers has gained a reputation among New York society through word of mouth, it remains one of New York's hidden secrets.

## Flowers and Décor

Décor could very well be one of the most fun parts of the entire wedding planning process. Regardless of how big, small, lavish, or low-key your wedding is, you have a special opportunity to reflect your own personal style though your décor. Every item – from the flowers to the candles– gives you a chance to make your wedding décor memorable and uniquely yours. Here are some of the top New York City event décor companies, many of which I've had the great pleasure of working with in the past.

## Tantawan Bloom

Tantawan Bloom is a New York-based floral company that infuses Thai-inspired technique and aesthetic. Although its most popular service is exquisite, high-end wedding floral design, it also offers planning and full event production services. Tantawan Bloom has been recognized in many

Tantawan Bloom created this stunning floral escort card setup for an Edison Ballroom couple. 67

top wedding publications, including New York Magazine, The Knot Wedding Magazine, In Style Wedding Magazine, Brides Magazine, and Grace Ormond Wedding Style Magazine.

## Swank Productions

Swank Productions is a planning, design, and production company that specializes in one-of-a-kind, luxury party and event experiences. With a strong belief that no event should be done twice, Swank Productions is known for its beyond-the-box design and flawless execution. Swank Productions has been recognized in a number of wedding publications and was voted "Best of the Best" by The Knot. The Wedding Industry Survey Network (WISN) also named Swank Productions' CEO Maya Kalman to its advisory board in order to fill the need for timely and accurate information in the wedding business. Swank Productions is a favorite of Edison Ballroom clients, and we are always impressed with their stunning work.

## Diana Gould Ltd.

Diana Gould Ltd. is a high-end floral design and event décor company specializing in complete room décor for all types of private events. Working in the events industry for over two decades, Diana Gould Ltd. is renowned for its innovation in design and execution. The company provides clients with services for nearly all of their event needs, including floral design, custom table linen and fabric, rentals, custom-made furniture and props, ambient lighting and pin-spotting, and in-house graphic design and printing services. I have had the pleasure of working with owner Jen Gould on many events over the years.

## DeJuan Stroud

DeJuan Stroud is an event design business located in Tribeca, New York City. Owner Dejuan Stroud, driven by his passion and love for flowers, left Wall Street in 1996 to found the company with his wife Debra. Stroud is well known among celebrities and New Yorkers in society and politics. He has been a featured expert on Martha Stewart Radio, CBS, NBC, WE, and Oxygen Network. Stroud's work has also been featured in several wedding publications, including Martha Stewart Weddings, Modern Bride, Grace Ormond Wedding Style, New York Magazine, and Elegant Bride.

## Interview with Golf Srithamrong, Lead Designer at Tantawan Bloom

**The last time I saw your floral arrangements at the Edison Ballroom I felt like I was in a fairy tale. How many flowers did you use for this event?**

For the arrangements created for Sara and Nick's wedding at the Edison Ballroom, we used many different kinds of roses and spray roses in shades of white, ivory, butter cream and blush. We used more than 8000 stems of roses, more than 1200 stems of white and green hydrangeas, more than 500 stems of white Phalaenopsis orchids, over 1200 stems of peony in blush and white, many ranunculus and many other flowers.

**How long does it take to transform a room like you did for that wedding?**

We arrived to the Edison ballroom at 8 am and we finished and were ready for ceremony by 7pm. We did have to flip the room, however, which took another hour afterwards, so it was about 8 full hours, nearly 9 hours that day to set up. Most of our work had been prepared at our warehouse since that Tuesday, having worked Tuesday, Wednesday and Thursday in preparation. During those days we condition every single stem: clean and place them in the appropriate temperature water, as well as prepare the mechanics, hardgoods, etc. The day prior to the wedding we worked a full 8 hours creating the arrangements.

**Tell me about your flowers, where are they coming from? I hear most flowers come from South America...**

More than 85% of the roses and hydrangeas we use are brought in from Colombia and Ecuador. Our orchids are imported from Thailand and Holland. The peonies and ranunculus are from France, Italy and from a local grower here in United States, and our cherry blossoms are from a local grower as well.

**Can you tell me a bit about the price range of your arrangements?**

Our centerpieces ranged in price that day from 550 -1500 US dollars.

**What's is your most requested flower for weddings?**

Mostly orchids, roses then hydrangeas.

## Atlas Floral Decorators

Atlas Floral Decorators is a New York-based family-owned and operated business that started in 1945. It began as a small store on Flatbush Avenue in Brooklyn and has since grown into a national corporation with entities in several states and countries. Atlas provides décor for events of all sizes, supplying items like floral decorations, linen, props, lighting, and more. Over the years, Atlas has gained an excellent reputation among high-end clients, designing flowers for Presidents, the Trump Family, and members of the motion picture industry.

Special Tip: I chose Atlas Floral Decorators for my wedding and I could not have been happier with their work. I've known of Atlas for years and they been a true favorite among many Edison Ballroom clients for their professionalism and original work. I had the pleasure of working with Matthew Kolins for my wedding — his creativity and industry experience helped bring my vision for my wedding to life!

## Cake

No traditional wedding is complete without the cake. The cutting of the cake symbolizes good fortune for the newly married couple. For this reason, the wedding cake and cake-cutting ceremony has long-been regarded as an important part of the wedding reception. Here are a few of the top New York wedding cake designers.

## Cake Alchemy

Cake Alchemy confections fuse together flavor, design, and ambience to create edible works of art. Owner Lauri Ditunno, a Food Network Challenge participant, was featured on WE TVs Amazing Wedding Cakes and has been recognized in a number of wedding magazine publications. Cake Alchemy creates truly memorable cakes for its bride and grooms, using only the finest ingredients and handcrafted detailed decorations.

Atlas created this stunning table setup for my winter wedding at Edison Ballroom.

Here is the custom escort table that Atlas created to match my red wedding décor.

Sylvia Weinstock Cakes created this posh cake for an Edison Ballroom couple.

## Sylvia Weinstock Cakes

Sylvia Weinstock is known as the "Leonardo da Vinci of wedding cakes." Her legendary cakes have made her a top dessert designer among the rich and famous, with Oprah Winfrey, Robert Di Niro, J.Lo, and the Clintons among some of her past clients. Weinstock uses only the finest ingredients to ensure that every client receives a fresh, moist cake and delicious work of art. Whether you're looking for a cake with exquisite floral design, or one that represents your personal story, Sylvia Weinstock Cakes can handle it all!

### Interview with Sylvia Weinstock, Founder of Sylvia Weinstock Cakes

**I think one of the highlights of every wedding is the cutting of the cake, why do you think people love that part so much?**

The cutting of the wedding cake is the first thing a newly married couple does together. It symbolizes caring for each other and shares the sweetness of the marriage with the guests

**What was the biggest cake you ever created?**

Perhaps the biggest and largest cake to date was for 3000 guests.

**What is the most popular cake now, is taller always better?**

The most popular cake is still the classic. Chocolate or yellow butter cake. Some brides want red velvet or carrot cake but the classic wins out most of the time. The size of the cake should be appropriate for the occasion as well as the site of the event. A tall cake in a low ceiling room does not work.

**What is the price range of your cakes?**

As to price, it depends on design and art work. Labor is the issue.

**Do you have a secret recipe?**

I have no secret recipes except to use the finest and best ingredients available and to be proud of our product, which carries our name.

## Ron Ben-Israel Cakes

Ron Ben-Israel Cakes has an excellent reputation in the industry. The New York Times has referred to Ron Ben-Israel as "the Manolo Blahnik of wedding cakes," and the highly regarded Zagat survey named him "the wedding cake master." Ron Ben-Israel's specialty and wedding creations have been featured in a variety of national publications, including Town & Country and New York Magazine. The company was also featured in the "Vera Wang on Weddings" book.

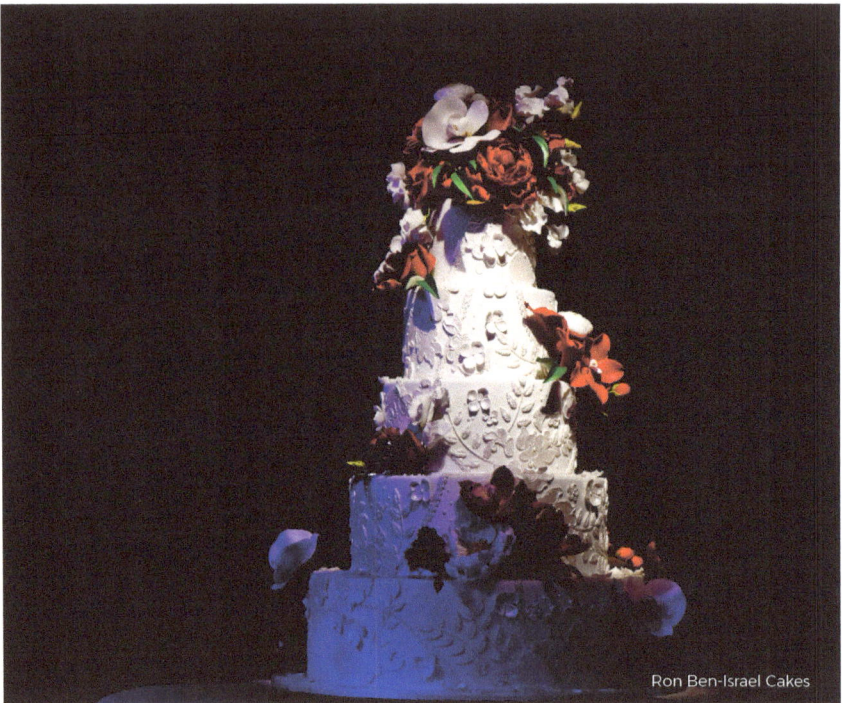

Ron Ben-Israel Cakes

Special Tip: I used Ron Ben-Israel for my wedding and the cake was not only stunning, but it was also delicious! The red flowers matched my décor and the lace design matched my Galia Lahav bridal gown. I highly recommend Ron Ben-Israel Cakes for your wedding – his work exceeded my expectations in every way. Make sure to take advantage of the cake tasting that is offered – it was fun, filling, and extremely informative!

***

For the sake of space, this section features only a few wedding vendors per category. I've had the great pleasure of working with many of these vendors and can verify the outstanding quality of their work. However, it is important to keep in mind that there are many other phenomenal wedding vendors out there. Plenty of great event planners, musicians, photographers, décor companies, and wedding cake bakeries did not make it into this chapter. For more New York wedding vendors, take a look at the resource section at the back of this book – it includes hundreds of amazing vendors and was designed to help all brides with varying styles and budgets. I promise it will be a very useful resource in helping you plan your ultimate New York wedding!

# BONUS CHAPTER

## The Hamptons

# Bonus Chapter:
# The Hamptons

Only a few hours outside Manhattan, the Hamptons has long been a popular spot for fabulous New York weddings. In this Bonus Chapter, I cover some of the top venues, caterers, and activities to help you plan the perfect Hamptons wedding.*

## Venues

### The Bridgehampton Tennis and Surf Club

Bordered by the Atlantic Ocean, Mecox Bay, and Sam's Creek, The Bridgehampton Tennis and Surf Club is a fantastic option to host your wedding. This private tennis and beach club offers a 1,200 ft. private beach to hold your ceremony, while its formal ballroom accommodates up to 200 guests for a seated dinner. Along with the beautiful scenery, your guests can enjoy The Bridgehampton Tennis and Surf Club's delicious food, which is catered by the well-known Robbins Wolfe Eventeurs.

### The Southampton Inn

Located in Southampton Village, The Southampton Inn is a popular private event space for weddings. Its ballroom can accommodate up to 150 guests for a seated dinner, with the option to add an outdoor patio to accommodate an additional 125 guests. The hotel offers 90 guest rooms, a pool, tennis courts, and extensive lawns that can be accessed by all guests of the hotel.

### Oceanbleu

Oceanbleu at the Westhampton Bath and Tennis Hotel and Marina is a popular beachfront venue with views of the Atlantic Ocean. Couples can choose to have their ceremony on the beach or in the hotel's majestic ballroom. There is a bridal suite available on-site for newlyweds, and wedding guests can stay in

---

*For a full list of the companies covered in this bonus chapter, check out the resource section at the back of this book.

any of the eclectic guest rooms or beach cottages. Robbins Wolfe Eventeurs is the exclusive caterer for Oceanbleu. The venue does offer a Glatt kosher catering option for clients. Hotel amenities include tennis courts, a fitness center, and a private pool.

## Lessing's 360° East at Montauk Downs

Lessing's 360° East at Montauk Downs is a one-of-a-kind wedding destination. Its private event space overlooks beautiful sights, including breathtaking views of Montauk, one of the oldest lighthouses in New York State, and an 18-hole golf course designed by Robert Trent Jones. The venue can accommodate up to 350 guests for a cocktail reception-style setup and 225 guests for a seated dinner.

## Montauk Yacht Club

Montauk Yacht Club is the perfect place to host your special day. The venue has various indoor and outdoor options for your wedding. You can get married on the beach and hold the reception outdoors on The Great Lawn, which accommodates up to 1,000 guests. Or you can hold the reception indoors in the beautiful Farmhouse Ballroom, which accommodates up to 160 guests. In addition to wedding services, Montauk Yacht Club also offers on-site activities for wedding guests, including a spa, a private lake beach, pools, tennis courts, and paddleboard excursions.

## Navy Beach

Couples that are looking to have their wedding at a venue with a true Montauk feel should explore Navy Beach. The wedding ceremony and reception can take place on its 200-ft. private beach, or inside at the bar and dining room. Navy Beach's nautical-theme décor and contemporary style provides guests with a memorable Montauk wedding experience.

## Trumpets at the Gate

Trumpets at the Gate is a waterfront event space that is perfect for hosting your dream Hamptons wedding. This elegant and intimate venue accommodates up to 120 guests. Its wedding package includes cocktail hour, dining selections, top shelf liquor, wine, dessert, and a wedding cake.

### Gurney's Montauk

This beachfront hotel and resort is a popular Hamptons wedding venue. Gurney's Montauk has two well-designed decks for hosting an intimate ceremony and reception, and its beachside banquet hall can accommodate up to 220 guests. The hotel offers a variety of guest accommodations so that wedding guests can be entertained on-site. Also located at Gurney's Montauk is the world-class Seawater Spa, which is a perfect place to relax before your big day.

## Catering

### Peter Ambrose Events Catering

Peter Ambrose Events Catering, located in East Hampton, has 20 years of experience catering weddings. The company offers many different classic menu options and takes personal requests from clients into consideration.

### Food and Co.

Food and Co. is a catering company located in East Hampton with over two decades of experience. The company focuses heavily on the details of its menu and on the quality of ingredients used. Food and Co.'s sister company is a full-service catering company named Hampton Clam Bake Catering Company, which specializes in clam bakes and grilled specialties.

### Janet O'Brien Event Caterers

Janet O'Brien Event Caterers is a widely celebrated catering company in both New York City and the Hamptons. Believing that each event should represent clients' individual tastes, it offers customizable menus with unique and delicious options.

### Exquisite Food

Exquisite Food is a well-known catering company in the Hamptons. This creative boutique caterer provides the highest quality ingredients and service to its clients.

## The Art of Eating

The Art of Eating is a catering company in the Hamptons that emphasizes food presentation using the finest quality of ingredients. It believes it is important for guests to admire both the taste and appearance of food.

## Activities

Wedding planning can be tiring and time-consuming, so it's important to plan fun activities during your free time. Trust me, everyone needs a break from wedding-planning mode every once in a while! Here are some great activities in the Hamptons for you and your guests to enjoy.

### Outdoor Activities

Reserve a day for yourself where you can relax on the beach or partake in beach activities like paddle boarding, volleyball, and surfing. Boat cruises are also a great way to spend your day. If you are looking for a more adventurous outdoor activity, you can spend the day sailing at either Sail Montauk Sailing Charters or Sag Harbor Sailing – both are members of the American Sailing Association (ASA) and can accommodate any level of sailing experience.

### Hotel Activities

Many hotels in the Hamptons offer amenities like heated indoor/outdoor pools, saunas, spas, and fully equipped fitness centers. Check out the website of your hotel to learn more about the amenities for guests.

### Spa Day

The best way to de-stress before your wedding is spending a day at the spa. The Hamptons has many different spa options – try Spa MYC at the Montauk Yacht Club or Seawater Spa at Gurney's Montauk Hotel and Resort.

### Film Festivals

You may be able to enjoy the Hamptons International Film Festival or the Long Island Film Festival if your wedding dates overlap. Both of these festivals show independent films that express the different perspectives of people both locally and globally.

## Montauk Lighthouse

You can visit the famous Montauk Lighthouse – the oldest lighthouse in New York State and a national historic landmark. It is definitely worth taking a trip to see.

## Picnic

A relaxing picnic is always a nice idea! A great location for a relaxing, low-key picnic is The Great Lawn located in Westhampton Beach.

## Conclusion

Planning a wedding is a time-consuming and complicated undertaking that can overwhelm most people. I decided to write this book to help couples getting married in New York, making the whole process a little easier for them. The resource section at the end of this book is an invaluable tool for couples planning their wedding. It lists hundreds of wedding vendors across various industries, including everything from wedding planners to bridal hair and makeup.

Please contact me at michele@theultimatenewyorkwedding.com with any feedback. I would love to hear your thoughts and see how I can better help couples plan their ultimate New York wedding.

Best of luck to you in the wedding planning process!

Michele Lo Manto

# RESOURCES

# EVENT VENDORS

## Catering

## MANHATTAN

### Abigail Kirsch Catering

A renowned catering company that operates a select group of exclusive venues. It also has preferred relationships with vendors throughout the Tri-state area.

**Website**
abigailkirsch.com

**Contact**
Alison Awerbuch

**Email**
Contact through website

**Phone**
(212) 696-4076

**Address**
71 W. 23rd Street, Suite 1611, New York, NY 10010

### Appetite

A catering company that offers expertise in the events industry and has working knowledge of all aspects of event production.

**Website**
appetitenyc.com

**Contact**
Carolyn

**Email**
carolyn@appetitenyc.com

**Phone**
(212) 461-1455

**Address**
215 W. 29th Street, New York, NY 10001

### Between the Bread

A full-service event planning and catering company that offers clean, modern plate presentations.

**Website**
betweenthebread.com

**Contact**
Samira Mahboubian

**Email**
samira@betweenthebread.com

**Phone**
(212) 765-1840 ext. 315

**Address**
244 W. 54th Street, Suite 504, New York, NY 10019

### Blue Smoke Catering

This company caters events of any size and provides home-style menu options.

**Website**
bluesmoke.com/catering/

**Contact**
Malysa Volpicelli

**Email**
mvolpicelli@bluesmoke.com

**Phone**
(212) 447-7733

**Address**
116 E. 27th Street, New York, NY 10016

## Bukhara Grill

A catering company that uses both modern and traditional Indian recipes for its creative menu.

**Website**
bukharagrill.ypguides.net/

**Email**
BukharaGrill49@gmail.com

**Phone**
(212) 888-2839

**Address**
217 E. 49th Street, New York, NY 10017

## Canard Inc.

A catering company that has redefined standards in food, service, and presentation for over 20 years.

**Website**
canardinc.com

**Contact**
Kelven Book: kelven@canardinc.com

**Email**
info@canardinc.com

**Phone**
(212) 947-2480

**Address**
503 W. 43rd Street, New York, NY 10036

## Catering by Restaurants Associates

A custom caterer that uses fresh, local and seasonal ingredients in all of its dishes.

**Website**
restaurantassociates.com

**Contact**
Nina Cochraneat

**Email**
info@restaurantassociates.com

**Phone**
(212) 757-0461

**Address**
Carnegie Hall, 130 W. 56th Street, New York, NY 10019

## Creative Edge Parties

A catering and event planning company with over 20 years of experience.

**Website**
creativeedgeparties.com

**Contact**
George Henderson: ghenderson@creativeedgeparties.com

**Email**
info@creativeedgeparties.com

**Phone**
(212) 741-3000

**Address**
110 Barrow Street, New York, NY 10014

## Darbar Catering Services

This catering company provides modern Indian cuisine and vegetarian options.

**Website**
darbarcateringservices.com

**Contact**
John Dass

**Email**
Contact through website

**Phone**
(646) 919-8989

**Address**
152 E. 46th Street, New York, NY 10017

## David Josephs Catering

A family business with over 20 years of experience in catering.

**Website**
davidjosephs.com

**Contact**
David Joseph

**Email**
joseph@davidjosephs.com

**Phone**
(212) 586-0654

**Address**
244 5th Avenue, Suite 200, New York, NY 10001

## Devi

An Indian catering company that diversifies its menu with international options.

**Website**
devievents.com

**Contact**
Kunal Lamba: kunal@devinyc.com

**Email**
info@devinyc.com

**Phone**
(212) 691-2100

**Address**
8 E. 18th Street, New York, NY 10003

## Diane Gordon Catering

An experienced, full-service catering company that offers custom menu design, décor styling, on-site staffing, and mixology services.

**Website**
dianegordoncatering.com

**Contact**
Diane Gordon

**Email**
info@dianegordoncatering.com

**Phone**
(212) 289-1230

**Address**
328 E. 117th Street, New York, NY 10035

## Esprit Events

A boutique kosher caterer known for its innovative menu that is prepared with fresh and seasonal ingredients.

**Website**
espritevents.com

**Contact**
Biana Novofastovsky

**Email**
info@espritevents.com

**Phone**
(212) 207-3220

**Address**
216 E. 49th Street, New York, NY 10017

## FCI Catering and Events

A full-service catering and event production company with the influence of world-renowned chefs at its fingertips. It is the exclusive in-house caterer and event producer for the International Culinary Center in NYC.

**Website**
fcievents.com

**Contact**
Alexis Fine Deangelis

**Email**
Contact through website

**Phone**
(646) 254-8581

**Address**
462 Broadway, 4th Floor, New York, NY 10013

## Food Trends Catering

A catering company that creates custom menus with locally-sourced, fresh ingredients.

**Website**
foodtrendscatering.com

**Contact**
Lara: lara@foodtrendscatering.com

**Email**
catering@foodtrendscatering.com

**Phone**
(212) 972-7320

**Address**
56 E. 41st Street, New York, NY 10017

## Great Performances

This full-service company offers catering, event planning and decorating services.

**Website**
greatperformances.com

**Email**
celebratefood@greatperformances.com

**Phone**
(212) 727-2424

**Address**
304 Hudson Street, New York, NY 10013

## Krisp Events

A catering company that offers an international, eclectic menu and encourages any customized menu requests.

**Website**
krispevents.com

**Contact**
Jedd Marras: (917) 922-4706, jedd@krispevents.com

**Email**
info@krispevents.com

**Phone**
(646) 775-4945

**Address**
244 Fifth Avene, Suite J283, New York, NY 10001

## Mari Vanna Restaurant

A catering service that offers a variety of classic Russian cuisine.

**Website**
www.marivanna.ru/ny/

**Contact**
Vella

**Email**
marivannanyc@gmail.com

**Phone**
(212) 777-1955

**Address**
41 E. 20th Street, New York, NY 10003

## Mary Giuliani Catering and Events

A catering company committed to sourcing the best food and beverage items in a down-to-earth, approachable manner.

**Website**
marygiuliani.com

**Contact**
Mary Giuliani

**Email**
info@marygiuliani.com

**Phone**
(212) 725-1658

**Address**
135 W. 20th Street, 6th Floor, New York, NY 10011

## Mint Catering

A part of the Tour de France NYC Restaurant Group.

**Website**
mintcatering.com

**Contact**
Julie Garrison ext. 100

**Email**
info@mintcatering.com

**Phone**
(212) 695-1169

**Address**
450 W. 33rd Street, New York, NY 10001

## Miss Elisabeth's Catering

A catering company that offers customized and diverse menu options using fresh, local, and organic ingredients

**Website**
misselisabeths.com

**Contact**
Elisabeth Weinberg

**Email**
elisabeth@misselisabeths.com

**Phone**
(917) 414-0512

**Address**
52 E. 13th Street, Suite 4A, New York, NY, 10003

## Newman & Leventhal

A Glatt Kosher catering company known for its exceptional food and cordial service.

**Website**
newmanandleventhal.com

**Contact**
Bert Leventhal

**Email**
bert@newmanandleventhal.com

**Phone**
(212) 362-9400

**Address**
45 W. 81st Street, New York, NY 10024

## Nova Catering & Events

This catering company can assist in menu development and all aspects of event production.

**Website**
novacateringco.com

**Contact**
Chris Barbier

**Email**
Contact through website

**Phone**
(212) 977-8900

**Address**
1140 Avenue of the Americas, New York, NY, 10036

## Olivier Cheng Catering and Events

A catering company that combines modern American cuisine with European and Asian flavors and hand-crafts menus to the personal tastes of its clients. It can also provide event consulting services.

**Website**
ocnyc.com

**Contact**
Olivier Cheng or Franck Cursat

**Email**
info@ocnyc.com

**Phone**
(212) 625-3151

**Address**
12-16 Vestry Street, New York, NY 10013

## Onegin

A catering company that caters events of any size and offers a variety of menu options.

**Website**
oneginnyc.com

**Email**
info@oneginnyc.com

**Phone**
(212) 924-8001

**Address**
391 Avenue of the Americas, New York, NY 10014

## Oysters XO New York

A catering company that views its cuisine as art and strives to make each event different than the last. It's sister company, PCK, is a Glatt Kosher catering service.

**Website**
oystersxo.com

**Contact**
Rifko Meier

**Email**
info@oystersxo.com

**Phone**
(917) 297-5929

**Address**
312 11th Avenue, Suite 22d, New York, NY 10001

## Peter Callahan

Catering company that views its cuisine as art and makes each event different than the last. Its sister company PCK is a Glatt Kosher catering service.

**Website**
petercallahan.com

**Email**
Contact through website

**Phone**
(212) 327-1144

**Address**
137 W. 25th Street, Suite 4, New York, NY 10001

## Pies-N-Thighs

This catering company has been recognized by the New York Times, New York Magazine, Daily News, and Food & Wine Magazine for its distinctive and delicious food.

**Website**
piesnthighs.com

**Contact**
Sarah Sanneh or Caroyln Bane

**Email**
Contact through website

**Phone**
(212) 431-7437

**Address**
43 Canal Street, New York, NY 10002

## PTL Events

A caterer that offers full-service catering and staffing.

**Website**
ptlevents.com

**Contact**
Caroline

**Email**
caroline@ptlevents.com

**Phone**
(646) 515-2326

**Address**
105 Pinehurst Avenue, Suite 2,
New York, NY 10033

## Relish Caterers & Event Planning

A full-service catering and event planning company that prides itself on its culinary innovation and impeccable service.

**Website**
relishcaterers.com

**Contact**
Samantha Lewis

**Email**
events@relishcaterers.com

**Phone**
(212) 228-1672

**Address**
830 Fifth Avenue, New York, NY 10065

## Riviera Caterers

An innovative catering company committed to carrying out the vision of its clients.

**Website**
rivieracaterers.com

**Contact**
Bobby

**Email**
bobby@rivieracaterers.com or
events@rivieracaterers.com

**Phone**
(732) 567-1316

**Address**
175 Varick Street, New York, NY 10014

## Robbins Wolfe Eventeurs

A catering and event planning company that offers all types of event services.

**Website**
robbinswolfe.com

**Contact**
Scott Fluntleyder: ext. 21 or
Bob Severini: ext. 14

**Phone**
(212) 924-6500

**Address**
25 Waterside Plaza, New York, NY 10010

## Shiraz Events

A caterer that offers Modern New American cuisine inspired by global trends and local ingredients.

**Website**
shirazevents.com

**Contact**
Angela Oh

**Email**
info@shirazevents.com

**Phone**
(212) 255-7001 ext. 18

**Address**
161 W. 22nd Street, New York, NY 10011

## Simply Divine Kosher Catering & Event Design

A full-service kosher caterer and event planning company.

**Website**
simplydivine.com

**Email**
info@simplydivine.com

**Phone**
(212) 541-7300

**Address**
334 Amsterdam Avenue,
New York, NY 10023

## Sterling Affair

A caterer that offers distinct stations with everything made from scratch.

**Website**
sterlingaffair.com

**Contact**
Josephine: jmelfa@sterlingaffair.com

**Email**
Contact through website

**Phone**
(212) 686-4075

**Address**
575 Madison Avenue, Suite 1006,
New York, NY 10022

## The Cleaver Co.

A well-known green caterer with a team of talented chefs and professional party planners.

**Website**
cleaverco.com

**Contact**
Kate Ferranti

**Email**
cleaver@cleaverco.com

**Phone**
(212) 741-9174

**Address**
75 9th Avenue, New York, NY 10011

## The Raging Skillet

This catering company has been voted as one of New York's top five wedding caterers by The Knot from 2009 to 2015.

**Website**
theragingskillet.com

**Contact**
Chef Rossi: chefrossinyc@aol.com

**Email**
Contact through website

**Phone**
(212) 677-2204

**Address**
335 E. Houston Street,
New York, NY 10002

## Thomas Preti Events to Savor

A reputable catering company with over 29 years of experience.

**Website**
thomaspreti.com

**Contact**
Jessica Alton

**Email**
info@thomaspreti.com

**Phone**
(212) 764-3188

**Address**
146 E. 37th Street, New York, NY 10016

## Tom Orlando Events

A company that has been providing unique catering services for all types of events for over 20 years.

**Website**
tomorlandoevents.com

**Contact**
Tom Orlando

**Email**
foodbuff@aol.com

**Phone**
(917) 750-1693

**Address**
212 W. 22nd Street, Suite 4K,
New York, NY 10011

## Union Square Events

This catering company works closely with its clients to make each events as unique and personalized as possible.

**Website**
unionsquareevents.com

**Contact**
Ron Parker

**Email**
info@unionsquareevents.com

**Phone**
(212) 488-1500

**Address**
640 W. 28th Street, New York, NY 10001

## Vai Catering and Events

A catering company specializing in contemporary Mediterranean cuisine with Italian influences.

**Website**
vairestaurant.com

**Contact**
Vincent Chirico

**Email**
info@vairestaurant.com

**Phone**
(212) 362-4500

**Address**
429 Amsterdam Avenue,
New York, NY 10024

# BROOKLYN

## Betty Brooklyn

A full-service catering company specializing in hand-crafted, seasonal cuisine. Offers professional staffing, bar service, party rentals, and day-of event planning services.

**Website**
bettybrooklyn.com

**Contact**
Nicole or Sam

**Email**
betty@bettybrooklyn.com

**Phone**
(718) 832-3889

**Address**
455 Utica Avenue, Brooklyn, NY 11203

## Cobblestone Catering

A catering company that can create customized menus for any kind of event.

**Website**
cobblestonecatering.com

**Contact**
Elizabeth: elizabeth@cobblestonecatering.com

**Email**
info@cobblestonecatering.com

**Phone**
(718) 222-1661

**Address**
199 Court Street, Brooklyn, NY 12201

### EVENTfull.nyc Catering

A full-service, off-premise NYC caterer that serves Manhattan, Brooklyn, and the Tri-state area.

**Website**
eventfullnyc.com

**Contact**
Melody Ozdenak

**Email**
melody@eventfullnyc.com

**Phone**
(718) 624-5777

**Address**
178 Atlantic Avenue,
Brooklyn Heights, NY 11201

### Naturally Delicious

A boutique caterer that offers seasonally inspired menus.

**Website**
naturallydelicious.com

**Contact**
Emily Sullivan

**Email**
info@naturallydelicious.com

**Phone**
(718) 237-3727

**Address**
487 Court Street, Brooklyn, NY 11231

### Fancy Girl Table

A full-service company that provides artisan catering and event design.

**Website**
fgtable.com

**Contact**
Jeanette Maier

**Email**
info@fgtable.com

**Phone**
(718) 422-9151

**Address**
294 3rd Avenue, Brooklyn, NY 11215

### Red Table Catering

A Brooklyn-based catering company that offers specialized menus.

**Website**
redtablecatering.com

**Contact**
Brooke Costello

**Email**
bcostello@redtablecatering.com

**Phone**
(917) 749-3639

**Address**
205 Leonard Street, Brooklyn, NY 12206

### Fig & Pig Catering Company

A creative catering company with a devotion to seasonal ingredients.

**Website**
figandpigcatering.com

**Contact**
Holly

**Email**
holly@figandpigcatering.com

**Phone**
(718) 233-4287

**Address**
217 Pulaski Street, Brooklyn, NY 11206

### Saucy by Nature

A farm-to-table boutique caterer specializing in Brooklyn-inspired food.

**Website**
saucybynature.com

**Contact**
Shayla Nastasi

**Email**
catering@saucybynature.com

**Phone**
(718) 789-0177

**Address**
884 Fulton Street, Brooklyn, NY 11238

## Sips & Bites

This catering company uses simple ideas and ingredients to create personalized menus for events.

**Website**
sipsandbitesnyc.com

**Contact**
Nicole: (718) 777-8080

**Email**
info@sipsandbitesnyc.com

**Phone**
(347) 889-5333

**Address**
178 N. 10th Street, Brooklyn, NY 11211

# QUEENS

## Cloud Catering

Caters events in NYC and the Tri-state area.

**Website**
cloudcateringny.com

**Contact**
Robert Crosby

**Email**
robert@cloudcateringny.com

**Phone**
(718) 383-3313

**Address**
42-81 Hunter Street,
Long Island City, NY 11101

## Prestige Caterers

A kosher caterer that uses fresh ingredients for its menus.

**Website**
prestigecaterers.com

**Contact**
Spencer Katz

**Email**
info@prestigecaterers.com

**Phone**
(718) 464-8400

**Address**
217-80 98th Avenue,
Queens Village, NY 11429

## Tip of the Tongue

A catering company known for its fresh, hearty dishes that are fancy without the fuss. Offers full-service planning and flexible custom menus.

**Website**
tipofthetonguenyc.com

**Contact**
Scott Fagan

**Email**
info@tipofthetongueny.com

**Phone**
(718) 693-2253

**Address**
11-32 49th Avenue,
Long Island City, NY 11101

## STATEN ISLAND ..................

### The Indian Clove

A catering company that blends Indian and Asian cuisine.

**Website**
indianclove.com

**Email**
write2us@indianclove.com

**Phone**
(718) 442-5100

**Address**
2071 Clove Road, Staten Island, NY 10304

## NEW JERSEY ..................

### Foremost Ram Caterers

This catering company was birthed when two well-known Kosher caterers merged to form an elite business.

**Website**
foremostcaterers.com

**Contact**
Jeffrey Becker

**Email**
Lisal@foremostcaterers.com

**Phone**
(201) 664-2465

**Address**
65 Anderson Avenue,
Moonachie, NJ 07074

## LONG ISLAND ..................

### Elegant Affairs

A highly reputable caterer and event planner.

**Website**
elegantaffairscaterers.com

**Contact**
Shobha Rao, Sharda Shenoy or Suman Pai

**Email**
Contact through website

**Phone**
(516) 676-8500

**Address**
110 Glen Cove Avenue,
Glen Cove, NY 11542

## WESTCHESTER ..................

### Le Moulin Event Planning & Catering

A catering company that customizes its menus to fit the needs and wants of its customers.

**Website**
lemoulincatering.com

**Contact**
Josyane Colwell

**Email**
josyane@lemoulincatering.com

**Phone**
(914) 591-4680

**Address**
75 Main Street, Irvington, NY 10533

# Decor

## MANHATTAN

### Bentley Meeker Lighting & Staging Inc.

A special events lighting company that provides design, service, and turn key production management.

**Website**
bentleymeeker.com

**Contact**
Creative Director
Scott Davis
sdavis@bentleymeeker.com
(212) 722-3349 ext. 223

**Email**
mail@bentleymeeker.com

**Phone**
(212) 722-3349

**Address**
465 Tenth Avenue, 2nd Floor,
New York, NY 10018

### David Beahm Design

This company offers custom event styling, design, and production. It does everything including iron working, floral artistry, and food styling.

**Website**
davidbeahm.com

**Email**
info@davidbeahm.com

**Phone**
(212) 279-1344

**Address**
529 W. 20th Street, Suite 11 West,
New York, NY 10011

### Blank Slate Events

A company that specializes in high-end floral design, styling and event planning.

**Website**
blankslateeventsny.com

**Contact**
Principal Owner and Event Planner
Anissa Burnett

**Email**
info@blankslateeventsny.com

**Phone**
(212) 706-8900

**Address**
225 W. 36th Street, Suite 505,
New York, NY 10018

### DeJuan Stroud

An elite design company specializing in opulant floral decor and event design.

**Website**
dejuanstroud.com

**Contact**
DeJuan Stroud, Owner

**Email**
info@dejuanstroud.com

**Phone**
(212) 431-9099

**Address**
348 W. 36th Street, New York, NY 10018

## Diana Gould Ltd.

A high-end floral design and event decor company with over 25 years of experience that specializes in complete room decor.

**Website**
dianagouldltd.com

**Contact**
Owner
Jennifer Gould
jennifer@dianagouldltd.com

Event Designer
Enza Anastasi
enza@dianagouldltd.com

**Email**
info@dianagouldltd.com

**Phone**
(212) 629-6993

**Address**
146 E. 37th Street, New York, NY 10016

## Lipari Production Group

A full-service special events production company that offers creative and comprehensive production services for events.

**Website**
lpgny.com

**Contact**
Founder and Owner
Chris Lipari

**Email**
info@lpgny.com

**Phone**
(212) 247-3331

**Address**
150 W. 47th Street, New York, NY 10036

## Martin Jobes Designs

A full-service boutique design and special events firm offering floral design, innovative prop design and fabrication, custom linens, lighting and customized graphics.

**Website**
martinjobesdesign.com

**Email**
info@martinjobesdesign.com

**Phone**
(646) 436-1528  or (212) 473-1378

**Address**
208 W. 29th Street, Suite 502,
New York, NY 10001

## Ovando

A full-service event design and production company that specializes in floral décor, customized furniture, decorative props and fabrics, lighting design and event coordination.

**Website**
ovandony.com

**Contact**
Director of Projects and Events
Bryan Roberts Hamecs

**LOCATIONS**
Madison Avenue
19 E. 65th Street, New York, NY 10065
**Phone**
(212) 988-2600
**Email**
madisonboutique@ovandony.com

Christopher Street
91 Christopher Street,
New York, NY 10014
**Phone**
(212) 924-7873
**Email**
christopherboutique@ovandony.com

## Stefan Event Décor and Floral Design

An event décor and floral design company serving the tri-state area for over fifty years.

**Website**
stefaneventdecor.com

**Email**
info@stefaneventdecor.com

**Phone**
(516) 239-2402

**Address**
149 Madison Avenue, Suite 203, New York, NY 10016

## Swank Productions

One of the leading event planning and design firms in the Tri-state area.

**Website**
swankproductions.com

**Email**
events@swankproductions.com

**Phone**
(212) 643-3211

**Address**
231 W. 29th Street, New York, NY 10001

## Taylor Creative Inc.

A company that provides an exclusive collection of modern furniture rentals for events.

**Website**
taylorcreativeinc.com

**Contact**
Allen Gorospe or Ethelie Aruoture

**Email**
info@taylorcreativeinc.com

**Phone**
(888) 245-4044

**Address**
150 W. 28th Street, Suite 1001, New York, NY 10001

## Tyger Productions

A full-service event design and production company offering services including floral design, lighting design and production, venue scouting, and event coordination.

**Website**
tygerproductions.com

**Email**
tygernyc@tygerproductions.com

**Phone**
(212) 382-4654

**Address**
1180 Avenue of the Americas, 8th Floor, New York, NY 10036

## Vineyard Wedding & Event Decoration

A full-service decor and centerpiece rental company serving the Tri-state area.

**Website**
vineyardeventdecor.com

**Email**
info@vinyardeventdecor.com

**Phone**
(646) 664-1047

**Address**
1441 Broadway, 3rd Floor, Suite 3076, New York, NY 10018

# BROOKLYN

## David Stark Design and Production

A full-service event design, planning and production company that specializes in custom decor, flowers, and every other aspect of event production, including venue selection, invitations, catering, entertainment, and integrated branding.

**Website**
davidstarkdesign.com

**Contact**
Project Director
Liz Holden

**Email**
info@davidstarkdesign.com

**Phone**
(718) 534-6777

**Address**
87 Luquer Street, Brooklyn, NY 11231

## MagicDecor

A wedding decoration company that specializes in canopies, wall and ceiling fabric decorations, special effects lighting, chandeliers, centerpieces, and decorative table and chair covers.

**Website**
magicdecor.net

**Email**
magicdecor@msn.com

**Phone**
(347) 604-1596

**Address**
2025 Schenectady Avenue,
Brooklyn, NY 11234

## Shades of Grey Productions Inc.

A full-service event planning and production company that specializes in cutting edge lighting, sound, staging and decor.

**Website**
Shadesofgreyproductionsinc.com

**Contact**
Owner
Morris Grey
morris@sogproductionsinc.com
(347) 386-1743

**Email**
Morris@sogproductionsinc.com

**Phone**
(347) 425-7244

**Address**
559 Van Siclen Avenue,
Brooklyn, NY 11207

# NEW JERSEY

### Ed Libby and Company
An event design company known for its award-winning florals, complete event design, and custom-built themed environments.

**Website**
edlibby.com

**Contact**
Ed Libby

**Email**
info@edlibby.com

**Phone**
(212) 339-9140

**Address**
205 South Newman Street, Hackensack, NJ 07601

### Evening of Elegance
An event design, floral design, and event planning company that specializes in South Asian wedding decor.

**Website**
eveningsofelegance.com

**Contact**
Dharmi Shah

**Email**
eveningsofelegance@gmail.com

**Phone**
(609) 273-1930

**Address**
P.O. Box 630, Princeton, NJ 08542

# QUEENS

### Adelisa Décor
A decor company that specializes in drapery, lighting, and custom-made wedding backdrops.

**Website**
adelisadecor.com

**Contact**
Jason or Adelisa

**Email**
info@adelisadecor.com

**Phone**
(347) 545-2293

**Address**
Richmond Hill, New York, NY 11418

# ONLINE

### Chuppah Rental NYC by Bella's Flower Shop
A service created by Bella's Flower Shop that provides wedding chuppah rentals for NYC and the Tri-state area.

**Website**
chuppahrentalnyc.com

**Email**
Contact through website

**Phone**
(347) 577-5300

### Your Chuppah NY
A company that provides quality, hand-crafted chuppahs at reasonable prices.

**Website**
yourchuppahny.com

**Email**
yourchuppahny@gmail.com

**Phone**
(646) 593-1960

# Event Planners

## MANHATTAN

### 6 Degrees of Celebration

An event planning firm serving the Tri-state area that offers both comprehensive and partial event planning services.

**Website**
6degreesofcelebration.com

**Email**
info@6degreesofcelebration.com

**Phone**
(212) 537-9485

**Address**
185 Madison Avenue, Suite 806, New York, NY 10016

### Amy Katz Events

A full-service event planning company that specializes in highly sophisticated, elegant events.

**Website**
amykatzevents.com

**Email**
Contact through website

**Phone**
(212) 535-8859

**Address**
1365 York Avenue, Suite 19E, New York, NY 10021

### A.A.B. Creates

A fully comprehensive creative design company that specializes in event planning and production services.

**Website**
aabcreates.com

**Email**
info@aabcreates.com

**Phone**
(212) 334-0005

**Address**
305 Broadway, New York, NY 10007

### Ang Weddings and Events

A boutique event planning company that provides personalized attention to clients throughout the entire planning process.

**Website**
angweddingsandevents.com

**Email**
info@angweddingsandevents.com

**Phone**
(646) 481-8078

**Address**
New York, NY

## Bellafare

A boutique event and wedding planning company that draws inspiration from interior design, fashion, art, and travel.

**Website**
bellafare.com

**Email**
events@bellafare.com
info@bellafare.com

**Phone**
(212) 216-9106

**Address**
853 Broadway, Suite 1118,
New York, NY 10003

## Colin Cowie Celebrations

A team of highly regarded event planners that have been at the forefront of wedding and event planning for over 20 years.

**Website**
colincowie.com/weddings

**Email**
info@colincowie.com

**Phone**
(212) 396-9007

**Address**
256 W. 36th Street, 4th Floor,
New York, NY 10018

## Brilliant Event Planning

An event planning company that simplifies the design and event planning process.

**Website**
brillianteventplanning.com

**Email**
sarah@brillianteventplanning.com

**Phone**
(917) 974-4729

**Address**
419 Lafayette Street, 4th Floor,
New York, NY 10003

## Cristina Verger Events

A full-service event planning company with expertise in event planning and production.

**Website**
cristinaverger.com

**Email**
cristina@cristinaverger.com

**Phone**
(212) 715-0590

**Address**
Seagram Building,
375 Park Avenue,
Suite 2607, New York, NY 10152

## Christine Paul Events

A full-service event planning firm that helps with venue selection, contract negotiations, event design, styling, photography, day-of coordination, and more.

**Website**
christinepaulevents.com

**Email**
info@christinepaulevents.com

**Phone**
(212) 220-9433

**Address**
340 Madison Avenue, 19th Floor,
New York, NY 10173

## Curtain Up Events

An event planning company that specializes in weddings of any size. Its services include set decoration, lighting, production, timing, and day-of coordination.

**Website**
curtainupevents.com

**Email**
info@curtainupevents.com

**Phone**
(212) 781-6390

**Address**
New York, NY

### Daughter of Design
A boutique wedding planning firm that brings a downtown approach to classic wedding traditions.

**Website**
daughterofdesign.com

**Email**
info@daughterofdesign.com

**Phone**
(646) 595-9009

**Address**
244 Fifth Avenue, Suite A202,
New York, NY 10001

### Firefly Events
A full-service wedding planning and design company that takes care of all logistics for events.

**Website**
firefly-events.com

**Email**
info@firefly-events.com

**Phone**
(917) 921-6052

**Address**
195 Chrystie Street, Suite 809C,
New York, NY 10002

### David Reinhard Events
A small boutique event planning firm that collaborates closely on every detail of the event planning process.

**Website**
davidreinhard.com

**Email**
hello@davidreinhard.com

**Phone**
(212) 535-1520

**Address**
New York, NY

### Gourmet Advisory Services
One of the nation's leading event planning and party coordination consultancies that specializes in upscale events.

**Website**
gourmetadvisory.com

**Email**
hrk@gourmetadvisory.com

**Phone**
(212) 535-0005

**Address**
315 E. 68th Street, New York, NY 10065

### Erganic Design & Living
A full-service event planning, design, and coordination studio.

**Website**
erganicdesign.com

**Email**
info@erganicdesign.com

**Phone**
(212) 206-1503

**Address**
120 W. 28th Street, Studio 4H,
New York, NY 10001

### Pink Bowtie Events
A boutique wedding and event planning company that provides a full range of planning, coordination, and consulting services.

**Website**
pinkbowtienyc.com

**Email**
pinkbowtieevents@gmail.com

**Phone**
(646) 283-0422

**Address**
New York, NY

## Save the Date

A renowned special events company that assists in venue and vendor selection, planning, and production.

**Website**
savethedate.com

**Email**
events@savethedate.com

**Phone**
(212) 333-3283

**Address**
18 Harrison Street, Penthouse,
New York, NY 10013

# BROOKLYN

## Ashley M Chamblin Events

A Brooklyn-based event coordinator and design consultant offering everything from day-of coordination to full event design.

**Website**
ashleymchamblin.com

**Email**
Contact through website

**Phone**
(281) 814-8910

**Address**
100 Woodruff Avenue,
Brooklyn, NY 11226

# WESTCHESTER

## Victoria Dubin Events

A full-service event planning and design company committed to turning its clients' visions into reality.

**Website**
victoriadubin.com

**Email**
vicki@victoriadubin.com

**Phone**
(914) 682-8647

**Address**
19 Orchard Drive, Purchase, NY 10577

# Florists

## MANHATTAN ........................................................................

### Anthony Brownie Flowers and Events

This floral company offers complete floral and event design, as well as custom stationery design.

**Website**
anthonybrownie.com

**Contact**
Anthony Brownie

**Email**
ab@anthonybrownie.com

**Phone**
(646) 221-8901

**Address**
120 W. 28th Street, Suite 4G,
New York, NY 10001

### Atlas Floral Decorators

A family owned and operated floral design and decoration company for events of all sizes. It provides all decor, including linen, props and lighting.

**Website**
atlasfloral.com

**Contact**
Matthew Kolins

**Email**
Contact through website

**Phone**
(212) 707-8355

**Address**
200 W. 57th Street, Suite 202,
New York, NY 10019

### B Floral

A floral company that specializes in personalized arrangements for private events of any size.

**Website**
bfloral.com

**Contact**
Founder and Lead Designer
Bronwen Smith

**Email**
info@bfloral.com

**Phone**
(646) 216-3169

**Address**
153 W. 27th Street, Suite 1002,
New York, NY 10001

### Belle Fleur

A renowned NYC floral and event design firm.

**Website**
bellefleurny.com/floral/weddings

**Contact**
Founder
Meredith Waga Perez
meredith@bellefleurny.com

**Email**
Contact through website

**Phone**
(212) 254-8703

**Address**
134 Fifth Avenue, New York, NY 10011

## Blank Slate Events
A company that specializes in high-end floral design, styling and event planning.

**Website**
blankslateeventsny.com

**Contact**
Principal Owner and Event Planner
Anissa Burnett

**Email**
info@blankslateeventsny.com

**Phone**
(212) 706-8900

**Address**
225 W. 36th Street, Suite 505,
New York, NY 10018

## Bride and Blossom
This company provides full-service floral design and decor, including bouquets, ceremony designs, ceremony structures, reception arrangements, complementary linens, draping, and accent decor.

**Website**
brideandblossom.com

**Contact**
Director of Events
Elianna Phelps

**Email**
info@brideandblossom.com

**Phone**
(646) 706-7783

**Address**
969 Third Avenue, 3rd Floor, Suite 4,
New York, NY 10022

## City Blossoms
A family-owned and operated floral and event company with over 25 years of experience.

**Website**
cityblossoms.com

**Contact**
Owner
Inna Lipovsky
Owner
Katrina Granin

**Email**
sales@cityblossoms.com

### LOCATIONS
Trinity Place
62 Trinity Place, New York, NY 10006
**Phone**
(212) 346-0756

46th Street
312 E. 46th Street, New York, NY 10017
**Phone**
(212) 867-5964

## City Iris
A floral design studio that also provides wedding invitations, lighting, linens and rentals.

**Website**
cityiris.net

**Contact**
Patrick Matrinez: cityiris@gmail.com

**Email**
Contact through website

**Phone**
(646) 684-4051

**Address**
37 W. 26th Street, Suite 200,
New York, NY 10010

## David Beahm Design

This company offers custom event styling, design, and production. It does everything including iron working, floral artistry, and food styling.

**Website**
davidbeahm.com

**Email**
info@davidbeahm.com

**Phone**
(212) 279-1344

**Address**
529 W. 20th Street, Suite 11 West, New York, NY 10011

## Diana Gould Ltd.

A high-end floral design and event decor company with over 25 years of experience that specializes in complete room decor.

**Website**
dianagouldltd.com

**Contact**
Owner
Jennifer Gould
jennifer@dianagouldltd.com

Event Designer
Enza Anastasi
enza@dianagouldltd.com

**Email**
info@dianagouldltd.com

**Phone**
(212) 629-6993

**Address**
146 E. 37th Street, New York, NY 10016

## DeJuan Stroud

An elite design company specializing in opulant floral decor and event design.

**Website**
dejuanstroud.com

**Contact**
Owner
DeJuan Stroud

**Email**
info@dejuanstroud.com

**Phone**
(212) 431-9099

**Address**
348 W. 36th Street, New York, NY 10018

## fleurs BELLA

An exclusive, eco-friendly floral design and decor company that creates every installation with its clients' desires in mind.

**Website**
fleursbella.com

**Contact**
Business Manager
Susan Silverman
susan@fleursbella.com

**Email**
Contact through website

**Phone**
(646) 602-7037

**Address**
55 E. 11th Street, New York, NY 10003

## Floraculture LLC

An affordable floral company with over 30 years of experience. Its unique relationships with wholesalers and farms around the world enables it to provide the high quality flowers at competitive prices.

**Website**
weddingsandeventsbyfloraculturenyc.com

**Contact**
Owner
Brian McNamara
floraculture@yahoo.com

**Email**
floraculture@yahoo.com

**Phone**
(212) 594-8600

**Address**
151 W. 28th Street, New York, NY 10001

## Francois-Pijuan

A floral design company that incorporates lighting, linens, furniture, and room decor into the event design.

**Website**
francois-pijuan.com

**Email**
info@francois-pijuan.com

**Phone**
(212) 591-6639

**Address**
150 W. 28th Street, Studio 1502B,
New York, NY 10001

## Lucy Wu Floral Design

A floral design company that specializes in silk flowers and wedding day arrangements.

**Website**
lucywu.com

**Contact**
Owner
Lucy Wu

**Email**
wedding@lucywu.com or
event@lucywu.com

**Phone**
(718) 675-9288

**Address**
112 W. 34th Street, 18th Floor,
New York, NY 10120

## Madison Florist

A floral company that also provides rentals and event coordination services.

**Website**
weddingsbymadison.com

**Contact**
Robert Agge, Manager

**Email**
Contact through website

**Phone**
(212) 686-5300

**Address**
315 Madison Avenue, Suite 901,
New York, NY 10017

## Martin Jobes Designs

A full-service boutique design and special events firm offering floral design, innovative prop design and fabrication, custom linens, lighting and customized graphics.

**Website**
martinjobesdesign.com

**Email**
info@martinjobesdesign.com

**Phone**
(646) 436-1528  or (212) 473-1378

**Address**
208 W. 29th Street, Suite 502,
New York, NY 10001

## Ovando

A full-service event design and production company that specializes in floral décor, customized furniture, decorative props and fabrics, lighting design and event coordination.

**Website**
ovandony.com

**Contact**
Director of Projects and Events
Bryan Roberts Hamecs

### LOCATIONS
Madison Avenue
19 E. 65th Street, New York, NY 10065
**Phone**
(212) 988-2600
**Email**
madisonboutique@ovandony.com

Christopher Street
91 Christopher Street,
New York, NY 10014
**Phone**
(212) 924-7873
**Email**
christopherboutique@ovandony.com

## Rountree Flowers

A floral company specializing in events that provides all event decor, styling, and related services.

**Website**
rountreeflowers.com

**Contact**
Founder
Jessie Weidinger

**Email**
info@rountreeflowers.com

**Phone**
(917) 209-7170

**Address**
1140 Broadway, Suite 901,
New York, NY 10001

## Tantawan Bloom

A high-end floral design, event decor, and full-production services company that infuses modern design with Thai inspired technique and aesthetic.

**Website**
tantawanbloom.com

**Contact**
Event Design Executive
Laura Lynch
laura.lynch@tantawanbloom.com

**Email**
info@tantawanbloom.com

**Phone**
(212) 564-0308

**Address**
31 W. 31st Street, New York, NY 10001

## Triplicity Flowers

A luxury florist that specializes in modern and creative floral design.

**Website**
triplicityflowers.com

**Contact**
Gloria Wu, Owner and Floral Designer

**Email**
info@triplicityflowers.com

**Phone**
(646) 535-8685

**Address**
120 W. 28th Street, Suite 4B1,
New York, NY 10001

# BROOKLYN

## Blossom and Branch

A boutique Brooklyn-based floral design studio that specializes in weddings and events in the NYC area.

**Website**
blossomandbranch.com

**Contact**
Owner
Sarah Brysk Cohen
(347) 422-7066
sarah@blossomandbranch.com

**Email**
Contact through website

**Phone**
(347) 422-7066

**Address**
970 Kent Avenue, Brooklyn, NY 11205

## Flowers by Reuven

A full-service floral studio that provides decor for weddings and events.

**Website**
flowersbyreuven.net

**Contact**
Reuven Latovitzki

**Email**
reuven.reuvens@yahoo.com

**Phone**
(718) 403-0369

**Address**
Brooklyn Navy Yard, 63 Flushing Avenue, Suite 601, Brooklyn, NY 11205

# QUEENS

## Cress Floral Decorators

A floral company with over 100 years of experience that specializes in wedding day flowers, lighting, draping, and linens.

**Website**
cressweddingflowers.com

**Contact**
V.P.
Lori Cress

**Email**
info@cressweddingflowers.com

**Phone**
(718) 423-6255

**Address**
248-02 Northern Boulevard,
Little Neck, NY 11362

## fLorEsta

A traditional floral design studio specializing in a wide range of romantic arrangements.

**Website**
florestanyc.com

**Email**
info@florestanyc.com

**Phone**
(347) 642-8108

**Address**
51-02 Vernon Boulevard,
Long Island City, NY 11101

# Photographers

## MANHATTAN

### A Day of Bliss Wedding Photography

**Website**
adayofbliss.com

**Contact**
Wolfgang Freithof
wolfgang@wfx.net

**Email**
Contact through website

**Phone**
(212) 724-1790

**Address**
307 W. 38th Street, Studio 1418,
New York, NY 10018

### Alex Kaplan
### Photo - Video - Booth Specialists

**Website**
twoweddingphotographers.com

**Contact**
Alex Kaplan
alexkaplanphoto@gmail.com

**Email**
Contact through website

**Phone**
(917) 992-9097

**Address**
New York, NY 10001

### Anthony Vazquez Photography

**Website**
anthonyvazquez.com

**Contact**
Anthony Vazquez

**Email**
info@anthonyvazquez.com

**Phone**
(212) 920-6082

**Address**
330 W. 38th Street, Suite 802,
New York, NY 10018

### Brian Dorsey Studios

**Website**
briandorseystudios.com

**Contact**
Brian Dorsey

**Email**
info@briandorseystudios.com

**Phone**
(212) 227-6772

**Address**
79 Reade Street, Studio 2C,
New York, NY 10007

## Dave Cross Photography

**Website**
davecrossweddings.com

**Contact**
Dave Cross

**Email**
dave@davecrossphotography.com

**Phone**
(212) 279-6691

**Address**
448 W. 37th Street, Suite 9B,
New York, NY 10018

## Edward Chan Photography

**Website**
edwardchan.com

**Contact**
Edward Chan
ed@edwardchan.com

**Email**
Contact through website

**Phone**
(646) 543-3201

**Address**
New York, NY

## Fred Marcus Studio

**Website**
fredmarcus.com

**Email**
info@fredmarcus.com

**Phone**
(212) 873-5588

**Address**
245 W. 72nd Street, New York, NY 10023

## Hechler Photographers

**Website**
hechlerphotographers.com

**Contact**
David Hechler

**Email**
studio@hechlerphoto.com

**Phone**
(212) 472-6565

**Address**
654 Madison Avenue, Suite 1509,
New York, NY 10021

## JayLim Studio

**Website**
jaylimstudio.com

**Contact**
Jay Lim

**Email**
info@jaylimstudio.com

**Phone**
(516) 333-0769

**Address**
307 W. 38th Street, New York, NY 10018

## John-Paul Teutonico Photography

**Website**
jpteutonico.com

**Contact**
JP Teutonico
jp@jpteutonico.com

**Email**
questions@jpteutonico.com

**Phone**
(917) 456-2371

**Address**
500 E. 77th Street, Suite 2022,
New York, NY 10162

## Jorg Windau Photography

**Website**
windauphotography.com

**Contact**
Jorg Windau
jorg@windauphotography.com

**Email**
jorg@windauphotography.com

**Phone**
(212) 781-8178

**Address**
307 W. 38th Street, 14th Floor,
Studio 1418, New York, NY 10018

## Julian Ribinik Photography

**Website**
julianribinikweddings.com

**Contact**
Julian Ribinik

**Email**
info@julianribinik.com

**Phone**
(212) 256-1646

**Address**
New York, NY

## Kenny Pang Photography

**Website**
kennypangphotoblog.com

**Contact**
Kenny Pang
kenny@kennypang.com

**Email**
kenny@kennypang.com

**Phone**
(917) 880-0959

**Address**
1178 Broadway, Suite 323,
New York, NY 10001

## Matthew Sowa Photography

**Website**
matthewsowaphotography.com

**Contact**
Matthew Sowa

**Email**
info@matthewsowaphoto.com

**Phone**
(917) 488-1989

**Address**
256 Canal Street, Suite 206,
New York, NY 10013

## Meg Miller Photography

**Website**
megmillerphotography.com

**Contact**
Meg Miller

**Email**
Contact through website

**Phone**
(317) 340-9036

**Address**
New York, NY

## Michael Jurick

**Website**
jurick.net

**Contact**
Michael Jurick

**Email**
photos@jurick.net

**Phone**
(917) 544-1871

**Address**
New York, NY

## Natural Expressions

**Website**
naturalexpressionsny.com

**Contact**
Owner and Director
Frank Ammaccapane
frank@naturalexpressionsny.com

**Email**
info@naturalexpressionsny.com

**Phone**
(212) 616-5008

**Address**
475 Park Avenue South, 30th Floor,
New York, NY 10016

## Patricia Kantzos Photography

**Website**
kantzos.com

**Contact**
Patricia Kantzos: patricia@kantzos.com

**Email**
patricia@kantzos.com

**Phone**
(212) 579-2550

**Address**
250 W. 93rd Street, Penthouse-E,
New York, NY 10025

## Salwa Photography

**Website**
salwaphotography.com

**Contact**
Anna and Simon Salwa

**Email**
contact@salwaphotography.com

**Phone**
(347) 744-8683 or (347) 744-8684

**Address**
New York, NY

## Sarah Merians Photography and Video Company

**Website**
sarahmerians.com

**Contact**
Director of Sales
Lisa
lisa@sarahmerians.com
(212) 633-0622

**Email**
info@sarahmerians.com

**Phone**
(212) 633-0502

**Address**
419 Park Avenue South,
Suite 1302, New York, NY 10016

## Steve Worth Photography

**Website**
steveworth.com

**Contact**
Steve and Kira Worth

**Email**
info@steveworth.com

**Phone**
(212) 986-5730

**Address**
244 5th Avenue, 11F,
New York, NY 10001

## True Love Wedding

**Website**
tlwedding.com

**Email**
info@tlwedding.com

**Phone**
(212) 567-0123

**Address**
4876 Broadway, New York, NY 10034

# BROOKLYN ....................................................................................

## Craig Warga Photography

**Website**
craigwargaweddings.com

**Contact**
Craig Warga

**Email**
craig@craigwarga.com

**Phone**
(917) 509-1764

**Address**
Brooklyn, NY 11215

## Le Image

**Website**
leimageinc.com/weddings

**Email**
info@leimageinc.com

**Phone**
(718) 971-9710

**Address**
254 36th Street, Unit 28, Suite C-448,
Brooklyn, NY 11232

## Peter Forman Photography

**Website**
peterbforman.com

**Contact**
Peter Forman

**Email**
peter@peterbforman.com

**Phone**
(347) 857-8707

**Address**
497 Henry Street, Brooklyn, NY 11231

## Susan Shek Photography

**Website**
susanshek.com

**Contact**
Susan Shek
susan@susanshek.com

**Email**
susan@susanshek.com

**Phone**
(347) 635-5577

**Address**
1 Northside Piers,
Brooklyn, NY 11249

## Tim Ryan Smith Photography

**Website**
timryansmith.com

**Contact**
Tim Ryan Smith

**Email**
info@timryansmith.com

**Phone**
(479) 790-7249

**Address**
65 Ocean Avenue, Brooklyn, NY  11225

## Windcatcher Photography

**Website**
windcatcherphotography.com

**Contact**
Chaomin "Chao" Tang, Event/Portrait
Photographer

**Email**
info@windcatcherphotography.com

**Phone**
(718) 759-8242

**Address**
Brooklyn, NY

# QUEENS................................

# NEW JERSEY .......................

## Christos Hountas
## (Speciality: Greek Weddings)

**Website**
christoshountas.com

**Contact**
Christos Hountas

**Email**
Contact through website

**Phone**
(718) 554-3122

**Address**
Bayside, New York 11361

## GK Photography
## (Specialty: Greek Weddings)

**Website**
gkphotographynyc.com

**Contact**
Gerry Katehis

**Email**
gk@gkphotographynyc.com

**Phone**
(718) 650-9573

**Address**
21-79 24th Street, Astoria, NY 11105

## Sarah Tew Photography

**Website**
sarahtewphotography.com

**Contact**
Sarah Tew

**Email**
sarah@sarahtewphotography.com

**Phone**
(917) 374-4346

**Address**
43-01 22nd Street, Studio 264,
Long Island City, NY 11101

## Amy Rizzuto Photography

**Website**
amyrizzutophotography.com

**Contact**
Amy Rizzuto

**Email**
amy@amyrizzutophotography.com

**Phone**
(276) 690-5343

**Address**
28 Janeway Place,
Morris Plains, NJ 07950

## Nayeem Vohra Photography and
## Cinematography
## (Specialty: South Asian Weddings)

**Website**
nayeemvohra.com

**Contact**
Nayeem Vohra
nayeem@nayeemvohra.com

**Email**
info@nayeemvohra.com

**Phone**
(856) 520-0344

**Address**
Cherry Hill, New Jersey 08003

## Pandya Photography
## (Specialty: South Asian Weddings)

**Website**
pandyaphotography.com

**Email**
info@pandyaphotography.com

**Phone**
(917) 740-0312

**Address**
70 Spruce Street, Suite 320,
Paterson, NJ 07501

# Music - Bands

## MANHATTAN

### 45 Riots

A collective of energietic NYC-based musicians that play current or classic music, including R&B, Funk, Hip-hop, House, Soul, Pop, Rock, Motown, Reggae, Jazz, Blues and inspired mixes.

**Website**
45riots.com

**Contact**
Founder
Adam Mason

**Email**
contact@45riots.com

**Phone**
(917) 969-0742

**Address**
New York, NY 10018

### Alex Donner Entertainment

Recently named one of the best entertainers in the country by the New York Times, these musicians play everything from Classical and Rock to Cabaret and Soul.

**Website**
alexdonner.com

**Contact**
Alex Donner

**Email**
info@alexdonner.com

**Phone**
(212) 752-2920

**Address**
330 E. 38th Street, Suite 23F,
New York, NY 10016

### Around Town Entertainment

An entertainment company that provides high-energy performances by bands, DJs and emcees. It can play any genre of dance music, including Motown, Rock, Disco, 80's, Big Band, Jazz, and Top 40s.

**Website**
aroundtownent.com

**Contact**
Founder
Adam Michaels

**Email**
info@aroundtownent.com

**Phone**
(917) 679-8636

**Address**
New York, NY

### Atomic Funk Project

A world-class party band that specializes in Motown, Soul, Funk and Dance hits.

**Website**
atomicfunkproject.com

**Email**
booking@atomicfunkproject.com

**Phone**
(800) 649-3865

**Address**
115 MacDougal Street,
New York, NY 10012

## Bud Maltin Metropolitan Music

This entertainment company has been providing live music and DJ services in the New York Metropolitan Area for over 20 years.

**Website**
budmaltin.com

**Contact**
Bud: bud@budmaltin.com

**Email**
Contact through website

**Phone**
(212) 447-6543

**Address**
New York, NY

## Element Music

An exclusive boutique production company that offers a wide range of talent and ensembles, including singers, musicians, dancers, and choreographers.

**Website**
elementmusic.com

**Contact**
Robin Ross: robin@elementmusic.com

**Email**
info@elementmusic.com

**Phone**
(212) 921-1080

**Address**
561 Seventh Avenue, Suite 802,
New York, NY 10018

## E Three

A production and talent collective based out of Times Square that provides live bands, jazz bands, string ensembles, and DJs.

**Website**
ethreenyc.com

**Email**
info@ethreenyc.com

**Phone**
(212) 354-6460

**Address**
37 W. 39th Street, Suite 1100,
New York, NY 10018

## Hank Lane Music

A full-service music and entertainment company that offers live wedding dance bands, ceremony musicians, classical ensembles, contemporary string groups, cocktail party musicians, professional DJs, photo booths, lighting packages and more.

**Website**
hanklane.com

**Email**
info@hanklane.com

**Phone**
(212) 767-0600

**Address**
65 W. 55th Street, Suite 302,
New York, NY 10019

## Jerry Kravat Entertainment

A New York City entertainment company that provides bands, DJs and classical musicians.

**Website**
jerrykravat.com

**Email**
info@jerrykravat.com

**Phone**
(212) 686-2200

**Address**
307 Seventh Avenue, Suite 1506,
New York, NY 10001

## Kinky Spigot and the Welders

These top-line musicians play great music with a hip, youthful edge. It specializes in Motown of the 60's, ground-shaking funk of the 70's, soulful R&B of the 90's, and eclectic indie songs of today.

**Website**
kinkyspigot.com

**Contact**
Band Manager
Yoni Rabino

**Email**
yoni@kinkyspigot.com

**Phone**
(914) 806-5844

**Address**
New York, NY

## Lucy Music

A boutique music company specializing in non-traditional wedding bands.

**Website**
weddingbandnyc.com

**Email**
bands@lucymusic.com

**Phone**
(718) 941-2295

**Address**
New York, NY

## Madison 35 Productions, LLC

A group of experienced singers and musicians that play Classic Rock, Soul, Motown, Jazz, Top 40, Rap, and an array of Jewish music.

**Website**
madison35.com

**Contact**
Vocals
Gena Zaiderma
gena@madison35.com
(917) 991-3440

**Email**
info@madison35.com

**Phone**
(917) 991-3440

## New York Edge Music

A New York wedding band that plays authentic Top 40, Hip-hop, Swing, Motown, and R&B.

**Website**
newyorkedge.com

**Contact**
Rich Greenfield
rich@newyorkedge.com
Shanti Rajah
shanti@newyorkedge.com

**Email**
info@newyorkedge.com

**Phone**
(212) 749-2364

**Address**
865 West End Avenue,
New York, NY 10025

## Silver Arrow Band

A wedding band from New York that specializes in up-tempo festival-style music. It can play everything from chart classics, Funk, Soul, Jazz, and Top 40 dance hits.

**Website**
silverarrowband.com

**Contact**
Rachel Madison

**Email**
info@silverarrowbands.com

**Phone**
(720) 937-5185

**Address**
New York, NY

## The Apollo Orchestras

A versatile Greek-American wedding band with over 20 years of experience.

**Website**
apolloorchestras.com

**Email**
tsifteteli@aol.com

**Phone**
(917) 495-2672

**Address**
New York, NY

## Star Talent Inc.

A boutique entertainment company that provides talented dance bands, DJs, ensembles, and entertainment through-out the New Jersey, New York, Connecticut, and Long Island.

**Website**
startalentinc.com

**Contact**
CEO
Michael Taylor
mtaylor@startalentinc.com

**Email**
info@startalentinc.com

**Phone**
(212) 541-3770

**Address**
590 Madison Avenue, 21st Floor, New York, NY 10022

## Veronica Martell Entertainment

An entertainment company that can provide any style of live entertainment for your event, from solo musicians to 40-piece orchestras.

**Website**
martellentertainment.com

**Contact**
Veronica Martell
veronica@veronicamartell.com

**Email**
veronica@veronicamartell.com

**Phone**
(914) 788-9587

**Address**
475 Park Avenue South, 30th Floor, New York, NY 10016

# BROOKLYN ...................................................................

### Elan Artists
A cooperative of musicians and artists that provide entertainment in New York, New Jersey and Long Island.

**Website**
elanartists.com/dancebands/
wedding-newyorkcity-ny.htm

**Email**
info@elanaartists.com

**Phone**
(888) 800-3526

**Address**
172 N.11th Street, Brooklyn, NY 11211

### MIXTAPE: A Cover Band for Hipsters
A band that set out to evolve a stagnant industry by offering fun, hipster for weddings.

**Website**
mixtapecoverband.com

**Contact**
Founder
Melanie Flannery
mixtapecoverband@gmail.com

**Email**
info@mixtape.nyc

**Phone**
(347) 750-6994

**Address**
Brooklyn, NY

### The Blue Vipers Of Brooklyn
An Early Jazz, Swing, and Blues band that specializes in songs from the 1920's and 1930's, New Orleans & Dixieland, Classic Blues, R&B and Western Swing.

**Website**
thebluevipersofbrooklyn.com

**Contact**
Chris Pistorino
chrispistorino@gmail.com
(718) 755-6016

Billy Nemee
maestro8995@yahoo.com
(347) 596-4406

**Address**
511 74th Street, Brooklyn, NY 11209

# STATEN ISLAND......

## LiveWire Entertainment
An independent band that plays everything from 1940's to today's hottest dance hits.

**Website**
livewireny.com

**Contact**
Anthony Furio

**Email**
Contact through website

**Phone**
(800) 757-3303

**Address**
17 Wolcott Avenue,
Staten Island, NY 10312

# NEW JERSEY ......

## Totally Live (Total Entertainment)
This company, which is part of the Total Entertainment family, provides sophisticated and fun live music for your wedding.

**Website**
totalentertainment.com

**Email**
info@totalentertainmentmusic.com

**Phone**
(201) 894-0055 or (800) 783-9335

**Address**
205 S. Newman Street,
Hackensack, NJ 07601

# Music - DJs

## MANHATTAN

### Classic Events Music

A DJ entertainment company that plays Top 200, Hip-hop, Classic Rock, Jazz, Pop, Alternative, Motown, Big Band, House, and Ethnic / Religious music.

**Website**
classiceventsmusic.com

**Email**
contact@classiceventsmusic.com

**Phone**
(646) 285-8631

**Address**
456 Park Avenue South,
New York, NY 10016

### DJ Johnny Stuart

A professional wedding DJ company with over 20 years of experience.

**Website**
johnnystuart.com

**Contact**
DJ Johnny Stuart

**Email**
info@johnnystuart.com

**Phone**
(646) 554-5148

**Address**
220 W. 24th Street, Suite 5F,
New York, NY 10011

### Expressway Music

A music production company founded in 1992 that has an experienced DJ roster. It can also provide live musicians, decor uplighting, photobooths and more.

**Website**
expresswaymusic.com

**Contact**
Event Coordinator
Charissa
Owner
Dave Swirsky

**Email**
info@expresswaymusic.com

**Phone**
(212) 953-9367

**Address**
10 E. 39th Street, Suite 1126,
New York, NY 10012

### FunkyGrooves DJ

A professional DJ agency founded in 1986 that provides customizable music entertainment services by experienced DJs.

**Website**
emmbangkok.wix.com/funkygroovesdj

**Contact**
DJ EmmBangkok, Founder

**Email**
pakdeez5@gmail.com

**Phone**
(202) 904-7902

**Address**
250 W. 50th Street, New York, NY 10019

## Generation Events

A full-service special event production company that specializes in DJs and live entertainment.

**Website**
generationevents.com

**Contact**
Owner: Jasion Fioto

**Email**
info@generationevents.com

**Phone**
(212) 505-7593

**Address**
63 E. 9th Street, Suite 3L,
New York, NY 10003

## Gotham DJ

A DJ company that plays a variety of genres to please different crowds, including Top 40 hits, Funk, Hip-hop, and 80s music.

**Website**
gothamdj.com

**Contact**
Founder: Andy Anderson

**Email**
gothamdj@gmail.com

**Phone**
(917) 593-9823

**Address**
New York, NY

## On The Move Entertainment

An event production company specializing in DJs, live music services, unique ensembles, and specialty acts.

**Website**
onthemove.com

**Contact**
Account Executive
Michelle Greenberg
michelle@onthemove.com

**Email**
Contact through website

**Phone**
(212) 229-1009

**Address**
210 W. 29th Street, 6th Floor,
New York, NY 10001

## Scratch Weddings

A DJ production company that employs the country's leading wedding DJs.

**Website**
scratchweddings.com

**Contact**
Wedding Sales Manager
Jenn (Dottino) Bedell
jenn@scratch.com

**Email**
weddings@scratch.com

**Phone**
(866) 955-8580

**Address**
36 Cooper Square, 2nd Floor,
New York, NY 10003

## White Label DJs

An entertainment company that provides experienced DJs for weddings.

**Website**
whitelabelweddingdjs.com

**Contact**
Owner
Nate Oinonen

**Email**
bookingwhitelabel@gmail.com

**Phone**
(617) 564-1404

**Address**
New York, NY

# QUEENS ......................................................................

## Seward Park Tech
A top-rated wedding DJ and lighting company serving the Tri-state area.

**Website**
dj.w3ddingdj.com

**Email**
info@Your.DJ

**Phone**
(855) 693-5669

**Address**
Ridgewood, NY 11386

# BROOKLYN ................................................................

## Beat Train Productions
A boutique DJ company that plays Big Band Jazz, Motown, Alternative, Indie, Hip-hop, Top 40 hits, and Electronic Dance Music.

**Website**
beattrainproductions.com

**Contact**
Founder
Ari Rosenfield
(508) 414-1113

**Email**
info@beattrainproductions.com

**Phone**
(347) 568-8987

**Address**
480 Humboldt Street, Suite 7B, Brooklyn, NY 11211

## Jarrell Entertainment
A full-service entertainment company that provides DJs, musicians, lighting, entertainment, and games.

**Website**
jarrellentertainment.com

**Email**
info@jarrellentertainment.com

**Phone**
(917) 449-3435

**Address**
83 11th Street, Suite 1, Brooklyn, NY 11215

## 74 Events
A DJ production company that plays any genre of music.

**Website**
74events.com

**Contact**
Founder/DJ
Gary Hoffmann (DJ Gaza)
gary@74events.com

**Email**
gary@74events.com

**Phone**
(917) 604-3970

**Address**
Brooklyn, NY

# STATEN ISLAND ...............................................................................

### Dash of Class Disc Jockey Entertainment
A hands-on, professional DJ service that specializes in music for weddings.

**Website**
dashofclass.com/site

**Contact**
Mike LoBasso or Joe Zicolello

**Email**
Contact through website

**Phone**
(718) 815-8900

**Address**
1250 Hyland Boulevard, Suite B1,
Staten Island, NY 10305

# LONG ISLAND ................................................................................

### More Than Music
The DJ and party entertainment division of Hank Lane Music. The company provides DJs, musicians, games, lighting, staging and A/V services.

**Website**
morethanmusic.biz

**Email**
info@more-than-music.com

**Phone**
(516) 626-9400

**Address**
200 Frank Road, Hicksville, NY 11801

# WESTCHESTER

## A Perfect Blend Entertainment

This DJ company offers professional DJ and emcee services, as well as uplighting, photobooths, flat screen TVs, and custom monograms.

**Website**
APBentertainment.com

**Contact**
Marie Mocieri

**Email**
celebrate@apbentertainment.com

**Phone**
(914) 941-0536

**Address**
21 North Broadway, Tarrytown, NY 10591

## Jimmy Dee Entertainment

A DJ production company with over 25 years of experience providing DJs, emcees, live music, lighting, video, and photography.

**Website**
www.jimmydee.com

**Email**
sales@jimmydee.com

**Phone**
(914) 428-9231

**Address**
78 North State Road,
Briarcliff Manor, NY 10510

# Specialty Entertainment Acts

## MANHATTAN

### Ali Luminescent
A circus performer, model, and teacher in NYC known for her fire dance, stilt walking, hula hoop dances, and more.

**Website**
aliluminescent.com

**Contact**
Ali Schmitz
alischmitz@gmail.com

**Email**
aliluminescent@gmail.com

**Address**
New York, NY

### Allen Dalton Productions
A unique entertainment production company specializing in one-of-a-kind acts, musicians and show-stopping events.

**Website**
allendalton.com

**Contact**
President
Allen Dalton

**Email**
Contact through website

**Phone**
(212) 935-4000

**Address**
157 E. 57th Street, Suite 2B
New York, NY 10022,

### Atomic Entertainment
An entertainment production company specializing in circus, dance, theatre, vaudeville, and the latest performance technologies.

**Website**
atomicentertainment.net

**Contact**
Aristic Director
Robb Wexler
robb@atomicentertainment.net

**Email**
info@atomicentertainment.net

**Phone**
(917) 583-5297

**Address**
New York, NY

### Barynya Entertainment
A Russian music, dance, and song ensemble established in 1991 that offers services like belly dancers, circus performers, ballet and jazz performers, violinists, Russian dancers, and traditional music ensembles.

**Website**
barynya.com

**Contact**
Owner
Mikhail Smirnov

**Email**
mikhail@barynya.com

**Phone**
(201) 981-2497

**Address**
New York, NY

## Cobblestone Entertainment Inc.

A full-service event planning company that specializes in unique and unusual talent for events, including musicians, belly dancers, harem girls, snake dancers, candle dancers, sword dancers, fire dancers, caricaturists, celebrity lookalikes, interactive dancers, living statues, magicians and more.

**Website**
cobblestoneentertainment.com

**Contact**
Susan Chagnon

**Email**
sc@cobblestoneentertainment.com

**Phone**
(212) 228-0602

**Address**
822 Greenwich Street,
New York, NY 10014

## Emphasis Entertainments

A talent booking company well-known for its experienced staff of professional break-dancers.

**Website**
emphasisentertainments.com

**Contact**
CEO
Gabriel Alvarez

**Email**
emphasisentertainments@gmail.com

**Phone**
(862) 262-8832

**Address**
New York, NY

## Flint & Cinder

A NYC-based performance duo offering sensual pyromantic entertainment.

**Website**
fortuneandflame.com

**Contact**
Flint Uskglass or Cinder Petrichor

**Email**
Contact through website

**Address**
New York, NY

## Giant Games of NYC

This company rents oversized outdoor games and carnival games, including giant chess, giant checkers, giant Connect Four™, giant Jenga™, and giant Scrabble™.

**Website**
giantgamesofnyc.com

**Contact**
Val: valdek2@verizon.net

**Email**
info@giantgamesofnyc.com

**Phone**
(917) 484-2704

**Address**
1540 York Avenue, New York, NY 10028

## Heliummm Aerial Dance

This company provides stunning aerialists for private events.

**Website**
heliummm.com

**Contact**
Chief Entertainment Officer
Heather Hammond

**Email**
heather@heliummm.com

**Phone**
(917) 280-2611

**Address**
New York, NY

## Karaoke Champ

A karaoke rental supplier.

**Website**
karaokechamp.com

**Contact**
Kaitlin: (888) 656-8889

**Email**
Contact through website

**Phone**
(888) 766-4776 or (212) 375-0091

**Address**
55 W. 21st Street, 3rd Floor,
New York, NY 10010

## KimLoveMuse Celebrity Psychic

A well-known Medium to the stars that can perform psychic readings for events.

**Website**
kimlovemuse.com

**Contact**
Kim Kamilla Nadir

**Email**
Kimlovemuse@gmail.com

**Phone**
(323) 683-6282

**Address**
125 W. 16th Street, 8th Floor,
New York, NY 10011

## Miss Fly Hips

A NYC-based acrobatic hoop dancer and fire performer.

**Website**
missflyhips.com

**Contact**
Karlie Dean

**Email**
karlie@missflyhips.com

**Phone**
(929) 269-6682

**Address**
New York, NY

## NY Drawing Booth

This company provides sophisticated 2-minute portraits hand-drawn by top artists using the latest technology. On-site is printing available.

**Website**
nydrawingbooth.com

**Email**
bookings@nydrawingbooth.com.

**Phone**
(347) 593-8663

**Address**
New York, NY

## Peter Straus & Co. Entertainment

A NYC-based company that provides high-quality, unusual entertainers for special events, including comedians, actors, circus performers, jugglers, mimes, impersonators and more.

**Website**
peterentertainement.com

**Contact**
Peter Straus

**Email**
pdstraus@gmail.com

**Phone**
(917) 805-8569

**Address**
420 W. 47th Street, New York, NY 10036

## Tom Kaufman Productions

This company has been providing quality, unique entertainment and production services to clients in the NY area for over 30 years.

**Website**
tomkaufam.com

**Contact**
Tom Kaufman

**Email**
tom@tomkaufman.com

**Phone**
(212) 223-0962

**Address**
155 East 55th Street, Suite 5A,
New York, NY 10022

# QUEENS

## Europa Sounds

An entertainment group that specializes in Greek-American music. It can provide DJs, emcees, lighting and AV, live musicians and decor.

**Website**
europasounds.com

**Contact**
Steve
steve@europasounds.com

**Phone**
(718) 938-5843

**Address**
152-53 Tenth Avenue, Suite 219, Whitestone, NY 11357

## Lea McGowan

A classically trained dancer, choreographer, professional aerial acrobat, and circus artist that provides fun, classy entertainment for events.

**Website**
gigsalad.com/lea_mcgowan_new_york_city

**Contact**
Lea McGowan

**Email**
lea.mcgowan@gmail.com

**Address**
Astoria, NY

## Jolie Henna By Nina

A henna artist available for private events that specializes in temporary henna tattoos and embellished body art.

**Website**
nyhenna.webs.com

**Contact**
Nina

**Email**
joliehenna@gmail.com or hennaparties@yahoo.com

**Phone**
(347) 351-6463

**Address**
2007 26th Street, Queens, NY 11105

## LMS Entertainment

An entertainment company that provides DJs, karaoke, stage and dancefloor lighting, photography, video recording and display, audiovisual services and decor.

**Website**
www.lmsentertainment.com

**Contact**
Jimmy Mousouroulis, President: jimmy@lmsentertainment.com

**Email**
info@lmsentertainment.com

**Phone**
(718) 229-7790

**Address**
200-01A 32nd Avenue, Bayside, NY 11361

# BROOKLYN ..........................

## Boris Rasin Arts & Design
A NY-based multimedia artist that creates quick, colorful drawings of guests for special events.

**Website**
borisrasin.com/event-portraits

**Contact**
Boris Rasin

**Email**
boris.rasin@gmail.com

**Phone**
(917) 657-2746

**Address**
645 East 26th Street, Brooklyn NY 11210

## Thrill Productions
A event production company that brings the newest, most cutting-edge products to events, including AIR graffiti, Virtual Hero Game, Video Flip, Graffiti Touch and Bobble Heads.

**Website**
thrillproductionsny.com

**Contact**
Eran Flek, Manager

**Email**
info@thrill-productions.com

**Phone**
(917) 968-0766

**Address**
41 Kosciuszko Street, Suite 125, Brooklyn, NY 11205

# NEW JERSEY ........................

## Total Entertainment Interactive
A company that specializes in all types of entertainment, including bands, DJs, multi-media, performers, and interactive games.

**Website**
totalentertainment.com

**Contact**
Phyllis

**Email**
info@totalentertainmentmusic.com

**Phone**
(201) 894-0055

**Address**
205 S. Newman Street, Hackensack, NJ 07601

# ONLINE ..................................

## Parties with Pizzazz Productions
An entertainment company that provides the latest and newest arcade, virtual reality, and casino games for private events. It also has music and decor divisions in-house.

**Website**
partieswithpizazz.tv

**Contact**
Nanci: nanci@partieswithpizazz.tv

**Email**
info@partieswithpizazz.tv

**Phone**
(516) 365-5064

# Transportation

## MANHATTAN..............................................................................................

### Highline Limousine

**Website**
highlinelimo.com

**Email**
Contact through website

**Phone**
(212) 335-0810

**Address**
270 Eleventh Avenue,
New York, NY, 10001

### NY Trolley Co.

**Website**
nytrolleyco.com

**Email**
info@nytrolleyco.com

**Phone**
(347) 410-1271

**Address**
244 5th Avenue, Suite D214,
New York, NY 10001

### Orbis Transportation

**Website**
orbistransportation.com

**Contact**
Founder
Eric Mirman

Founder
Scott Levinson

**Email**
info@orbistransportation.com or
sales@orbistransportation.com

**Phone**
(800) 878-2199 or (646) 374-4999

**Address**
244 Fifth Avenue, Suite 2056, NY 10001

### Regal Carriage

**Website**
regalcar.com

**Email**
ride@regalcarriageinc.com

**Phone**
(800) 331-5388 or (212) 244-2424

**Address**
18 West 33rd Street, New York, NY 10001

# QUEENS

### Churchill Executive Cars

**Website**
churchillexecutivecars.com

**Contact**
Jesse Sabo
jsabo@chruchillexecutivecars.com

**Email**
Contact through website

**Phone**
(646) 558-6303

**Address**
10-10 44th Avenue, New York, NY 11101

### Ecstasy Limousine Services

**Website**
aecstasylimousine.com

**Email**
customerservice@ecstacylimo.com

**Phone**
(718) 897-6108

**Address**
91-16 101st Avenue, Queens, NY 11374

# LONG ISLAND

### M & V Limousine

**Website**
mvlimo.com

**Contact**
Mark J. Vigilante, Founder

**Email**
info@mvlimo.com

**Phone**
(800) 498-5788 or (631) 543-0908

**Address**
1117 Jericho Turnpike,
Commack, NY 11725

# WESTCHESTER

### Silver Star Limousines

**Website**
silverstarlimo.com

**Contact**
Jeffrey Da Rocha or Freddy Ponciano

**Email**
info@silverstarlimo.com or
eventconsultant@silverstarlimo.com

**Phone**
(800) 640-2782 or (914) 476-3311

**Address**
47 Ash Street Yonkers, New York 10701

# STATEN ISLAND

### A-Class Limousine

**Website**
aclasslimosine.com

**Email**
information@aclasslimousine.com

**Phone**
(800) 760-7125

**Address**
2206 Hylan Boulevard,
Staten Island, NY 10306

### Black Tie Limo

**Website**
blktielimos.com

**Contact**
Anthony Tafuri

**Email**
info@blktielimos.com

**Phone**
(718) 980-5504

**Address**
60 Ashland Avenue E,
Staten Island, NY 10312

### Romantique Double Diamond Limousines

**Website**
romantiquelimos.com

**Email**
info@romantiquelimos.com

**LOCATIONS**
Staten Island
2041 Hylan Blvd.,
Staten Island, NY 10306
**Phone**
(866) 842-7965

Brooklyn
1421 86th Street,
Brooklyn, NY 11228
**Phone**
(866) 579-3155

# GREATER NY AREA

### GK Limo

**Website**
gklimo.com

**Email**
Contact through website

**Phone**
(845) 323-7533

**Address**
15 Bell Lane, Tappan, NY 10983

### K & G Limousine Service

**Website**
kgweddinglimo.com

**Email**
info@kglimo.com

**Phone**
(516) 437-3826 or (516) 437-3827

**Address**
244 Brooklyn Avenue,
New Hyde Park, NY 11040

# Venues - Traditional

## MANHATTAN

### Arena
A modern event space in Midtown Manhattan that was renovated in February 2013.

**Capacity**
Minimum Capacity: 60
Maximum Capacity: 600

**Catering**
On-site catering.
Outside catering is permitted

**Website**
arenanyc.net

**Contact**
Gina LaRochelle: gina@arenanyc.net

**Email**
events@arenanyc.net

**Phone**
(212) 278-0988

**Address**
135 W. 41st Street, New York, NY 10036

### Broad Street Ballroom
Located in Manhattan's Financial District, this venue had a long history as a banking hall in the early 20th century.

**Capacity**
Maximum Capacity Seated: 300
Maximum Capacity Standing: 550

**Catering**
No on-site catering

**Website**
broadstreetballroom.com

**Contact**
Donna Bradley, Special Events Manager

**Email**
info@broadstreetballroom.com

**Phone**
(646) 624-2524

**Address**
41 Broad Street, New York, NY 10004

### Capitale
Formerly the Bowery Savings Bank, this Stanford-white designed venue recently underwent a $1M renovation.

**Capacity**
Maximum Capacity Seated: 500
Maximum Capacity Standing: 1,500

**Catering**
On-site catering

**Website**
capitaleny.com/

**Contact**
William Curran
wcurran@capitaleny.com

**Email**
info@capitaleny.com

**Phone**
(212) 334-5500

**Address**
130 Bowery, New York, NY 10013

### Cipriani 25 Broadway
An Italian Neo-Renaissance inspired venue located in the heart of Manhattan.

**Capacity**
Maximum Capacity Seated: 550

**Catering**
On-site catering

**Website**
cipriani.com/en/services/
event-spaces/cipriani-25-broadway

**Email**
events@cipriani.com

**Phone**
(212) 499-0599

**Address**
25 Broadway, New York, NY 10004

## Cipriani 42nd Street

Formerly known as the Bowery Savings Bank, this national landmark building now operates as an event space and is conveniently located next to Grand Central Station.

**Capacity**
Maximum Capacity Seated: 850

**Catering**
On-site catering

**Website**
cipriani.com/en/services/event-spac-es/cipriani-42nd-street

**Email**
events@cipriani.com

**Phone**
(646) 723-0826

**Address**
110 E. 42nd Street, New York, NY 10017

## Down Town Association

A landmarked clubhouse that offers a variety of elegant venues for special events.

**Capacity**
Provided upon request

**Catering**
On-site catering.
Outside catering not permitted (except for cultural or religious purposes).

**Website**
thedta.com

**Contact**
Valerie Baker: v.baker@thedta.com

**Email**
v.baker@thedta.com

**Phone**
(212) 422-1997

**Address**
60 Pine Street, New York, NY 10005

## Cipriani Wall Street

This Wall Street venue, which has a long history in NYC culture, stands as a triumph of Greek revival architecture.

**Capacity**
Maximum Capacity Seated: 900

**Catering**
On-site catering

**Website**
cipriani.com/en/services/event-spac-es/cipriani-wall-street

**Email**
events@cipriani.com

**Phone**
(212) 699-4099

**Address**
55 Wall Street, New York, NY 10005

## Espace

A modern, versatile venue located in Midtown Manhattan.

**Capacity**
Maximum Capacity Seated: 550

**Catering**
On-site catering.
Outside catering not permitted (except for cultural or religious purposes).

**Website**
espaceny.com

**Contact**
Sales
Michael Rosenblum
mrosenblum@espaceny.com

**Email**
info@espaceny.com

**Phone**
(212) 967-7003

**Address**
635 W. 42nd Street, New York, NY 10036

## Gotham Hall

Originally constructed in the 1920's as the Greenwich Savings Bank, this venue is now a popular event space in Midtown Manhattan.

**Capacity**
Maximum Capacity: 500

**Catering**
On-site catering.
Occasionally allows licensed and insured outside caterers.

**Website**
gothamhallevents.com

**Email**
Contact through website

**Phone**
(212) 244-4300

**Address**
1356 Broadway, New York, NY 10018

## Liberty Hall at The Ace Hotel

A 2,500 square foot space located on the lower level of The Ace Hotel.

**Capacity**
Maximum Capacity Seated: 120
Maximum Capacity Standing: 200

**Catering**
On-site catering

**Website**
acehotel.com/newyork/event-spaces

**Contact**
Erin Brishnane: erin@thebreslin

**Email**
events.nyc@acehotel.com

**Phone**
(646) 214-5764

**Address**
20 W. 29th Street, New York, NY 10001

## Metropolitan Pavilion

Located in the Chelsea neighborhood, this venue offers 5 unique spaces that each have the feel of a New York City loft.

**Capacity**
Minimum Capacity: 20
Maximum Capacity: 1,500+

**Catering**
On-site catering.
Outside catering is permitted.

**Website**
metropolitanevents.com

**Contact**
Mariel
mariel@metropolitanevents.com

**Email**
info@metropolitanevents.com

**Phone**
(212) 463-0071

**Address**
125 W. 18th Street, New York, NY 10011

## Metropolitan West

Located in Hell's Kitchen, this completely renovated facility has two separate and adaptable event floors.

**Capacity**
Provided upon request

**Catering**
Information provided upon request.

**Website**
metropolitanevents.com

**Email**
info@metropolitanevents.com

**Phone**
(212) 463-0071

**Address**
639 W. 46th Street, New York, NY 10036

## Pier Sixty

The largest waterfront venue in Manhattan with views of the Hudson River.

**Capacity**
Minimum Capacity: 200
Maximum Capacity: 2,000

**Catering**
On-site catering

**Website**
piersixty.com

**Contact**
Meredith Barsky
barskm@chelseapiers.com

**Email**
events@piersixty.com

**Phone**
(212) 336-6144

**Address**
Pier 60, Chelsea Piers,
New York, NY 10011

## Prince George Ballroom

This Flatiron venue was recently renovated to modernize the historic space while maintaining its original Neo-Renaissance features.

**Capacity**
Maximum Capacity Seated: 300+

**Catering**
On-site catering.
Outside catering is not permitted.

**Website**
princegeorgeballroom.org

**Contact**
Ballroom Manager

Karen Jimenez
kjimenez@commonground.org
(212) 471-0870 ext. 2870,

**Email**
eventspaces@commonground.org

**Phone**
(212) 471-0882

**Address**
15 E. 27th Street, New York, NY 10016

## Rubin Museum of Art

An elegant event space with sophisticated architectural accents.

**Capacity**
Maximum Capacity Seated: 220

**Catering**
On-site catering.

**Website**
rmanyc.org/specialevents

**Contact**
Manager of Special Events
Olivia Cohen
(212) 620-5000 ext. 292

ocohen@rubinmuseum.org

**Email**
specialevents@rmanyc.org

**Phone**
(212) 620-5000 ext. 290

**Address**
150 W. 17th Street, New York, NY 10011

## Studio Arte

A raw, modern all-purpose loft space located in Midtown's Garment District.

**Capacity**
Maximum Capacity: 150

**Catering**
On-site catering.
Outside catering is permitted.

**Website**
jpoconcepts.com/venues/#studio-arte

**Contact**
Sales Manager
Jillian Egenberg

**Email**
info@jpoconcepts.com

**Phone**
(646) 558-5860

**Address**
265 W. 37th Street, 17th Floor,
New York, NY 10018

## The Current

One of New York City's newest water-front venues that offers an expansive open space with views of the Hudson River and Chelsea Piers marina.

**Capacity**
Provided upon request

**Catering**
On-site catering

**Website**
piersixty.com

**Contact**
Meredith Barsky
barskm@chelseapiers.com

**Email**
events@piersixty.com

**Phone**
(212) 336-6144

**Address**
Pier 59, Chelsea Piers,
New York, NY 10011

## The Edison Ballroom

This elegant, art deco inspired private event space opened in 2008 following a multi-million dollar renovation.

**Capacity**
Maximum Capacity Seated: 400
Maximum Capacity Standing: 1,100

**Catering**
On-site catering.
Outside caterer is not permitted (except for cultural or religious purposes).

**Website**
edisonballroom.com

**Contact**
Director of Social Events
Michele Wartski
michele@edisonballroom.com

**Email**
michele@edisonballroom.com

**Phone**
(212) 201-7650

**Address**
240 W. 47th Street, New York, NY 10036

## The Lighthouse

This waterfront venue, which has the feel of a sophisticated New York Loft Space, has views of the Hudson River and Statue of Liberty.

**Capacity**
Maximum Capacity: 800

**Catering**
On-site catering

**Website**
piersixty.com

**Contact**
Meredith Barsky
barskm@chelseapiers.com

**Email**
events@piersixty.com

**Phone**
(212) 336-6144

**Address**
Pier 61, Chelsea Piers,
New York, NY 10011

## The New Yorker A Wyndham Hotel

A cosmopolitan, art deco-style Midtown Manhattan hotel with a newly renovated ballroom.

**Capacity**
Maximum Capacity Seated: 360

**Catering**
On-site catering

**Website**
newyorkerhotel.com

**Contact**
John Yazbeck: jyazbeck@nyhotel.com

**Phone**
(212) 971-0101

**Address**
481 Eighth, New York, NY 10001

## The Plaza

A world-famous NYC hotel located on Fifth Avenue right outside Central Park.

**Capacity**
Maximum Capacity Seated: 500
Maximum Capacity Standing: 600

**Catering**
On-site catering

**Website**
theplaza.com

**Contact**
Social Sales Manager
Emily Reifel:
(212) 549-0506
emily.reifel@cpsevents.com

**Email**
Contact through website

**Phone**
(866) 770-8229

**Address**
768 Fifth Avenue, New York, NY 10019

## The Waldorf Astoria

A luxurious, world-renowned Park Avenue hotel with multiple venues on-site.

**Capacity**
Maximum Capacity Seated: 1,100

**Catering**
On-site catering

**Website**
waldorfnewyork.com/events

**Contact**
Director of Private Social Catering
Alan M. Shukovsky
(212) 872-4779

**Email**
Contact through website

**Phone**
(212) 872-4700

**Address**
301 Park Avenue, New York, NY 10022

## The Roosevelt Hotel

An iconic, elegant Midtown Manhattan hotel.

**Capacity**
Maximum Capacity: 375

**Catering**
On-site catering

**Website**
theroosevelthotel.com/weddings-rfp.aspx

**Contact**
Director of Catering and Conference Management
Bryan Kalman
bkalman@rooseveltnyc.com

**Email**
Contact through website

**Phone**
(212) 661-9600

**Address**
45 E. 45th Street, New York, NY 10017

## The Waterfront

Once a major West Side distrubution center, this industrial chic space is now used for private events.

**Capacity**
Maximum Capacity Seated: 500
Maximum Capacity Standing: 1,500

**Catering**
No on-site catering

**Website**
tunnelevents.com

**Contact**
Matthew Bieszard

**Email**
events@tunnelevents.com

**Phone**
(212) 695-8090

**Address**
269 Eleventh Avenue,
New York, NY 10001

# BROOKLYN

## Orion Palace
This venue features a grand ballroom on the main level and two halls on the second floor.

**Capacity**
Provided upon request

**Catering**
On-site catering

**Website**
orionpalace.com

**Phone**
(718) 375-1188

**Address**
2555 McDonald Avenue,
Brooklyn, NY 11223

## Passages
This unique restaurant located in the Sheepshead Bay area overlooks the piers and private yachts on the bay.

**Capacity**
Maximum Capacity Seated: 250

**Catering**
On-site catering

**Website**
passageny.com

**Phone**
(718) 368-3434

**Address**
2027 Emmons Avenue,
Brooklyn, NY 11235

## The Green Building
Originally constructed as a brass foundry in 1899, the building has since been converted into an elegant, mixed-use venue. Outdoor and indoor areas are available.

**Capacity**
Maximum Capacity Seated: 160
Maximum Capacity Standing: 300

**Catering**
No on-site catering

**Website**
thegreenbuildingnyc.com

**Contact**
Brooke Morris Rasheed
brooke@thegreenbuildingnyc.com

**Email**
info@thegreenbuildingnyc.com

**Phone**
(718) 522-3363

**Address**
452 Union Street, Brooklyn, NY 11231

## Wythe Hotel
The building of this Williamsburg hotel dates back to 1901, and now has six separate rooms that can hold events.

**Capacity**
Maximum Capacity Seated: 140
Maximum Capacity Standing: 250

**Catering**
On-site catering.
Outside catering not permitted.

**Website**
wythehotel.com

**Contact**
Sarah: events@wythehotel.com

**Email**
hello@wythehotel.com

**Phone**
(718) 460-8000

**Address**
80 Wythe Avenue, Brooklyn, NY 11249

# STATEN ISLAND

## Nicotra's Ballroom

This venue, located within the Hilton Garden Inn in Staten Island, can host events in the main ballroom or the outdoor garden area.

**Capacity**
Maximum Capacity Seated: 1,000

**Catering**
On-site catering

**Website**
nicotrasballroom.com

**Email**
Contact through website

**Phone**
(718) 477-2400 ext. 5

**Address**
1100 South Avenue,
Staten Island, NY 10314

## The Vanderbilt at South Beach

Staten Island's only oceanfront venue. Multiple rooms with indoor and outdoor options are available.

**Capacity**
Maximum Capacity Seated: 450

**Catering**
On-site catering

**Website**
vanderbiltsouthbeach.com

**Contact**
Sal Salutito

**Email**
Contact through website

**Phone**
(718) 447-0800

**Address**
300 Father Capodanno Boulevard,
Staten Island, NY 10305

# Venues - Non-Traditional

## BOAT

### Circle Line Sightseeing Cruises

**Website**
circleline42.com

**Email**
info@circleline42.com

**Phone**
(212) 563-3200

**Address**
Pier 83, W. 42nd Street,
New York, NY 10036

### East Coast Yacht Cruises

**Website**
eastcoastyachtcruises.com

**Email**
Contact through website

**Phone**
(800) 278-7178

**Address**
60 Chelsea Piers, New York, NY 10011

### Elite Private Yachts

**Website**
eliteprivateyachts.com/new-york-metro

**Email**
cruise.newyork@entertainmentcruises.com

**Phone**
(888) 957-2321

**Address**
Pier 62, Chelsea Piers, Suite 200,
New York, NY 10011

### Hornblower New York

**Website**
hornblowernewyork.com

**Email**
nycruises@hornblower.com

**Phone**
(646) 681-1799

**LOCATIONS**
Pier 40
Pier 40, 353 West Street,
New York NY 10014;

South Street
78 South Street,
New York, NY 10038

### World Yacht

**Website**
worldyacht.com

**Email**
contact@worldyacht.com

**Phone**
(212) 630-8100

**Address**
Pier 81, W. 41st Street,
New York, NY 10036

# MUSEUM ......................................................................................

## The American Museum of Natural History
One of the most architecturally magnificent and educationally rich venues to host a special event.

**Capacity**
Maximum Capacity Standing: 3,000+

**Catering**
On-site catering

**Website**
amnh.org/hostanevent

**Email**
hostanevent@amng.org

**Phone**
(212) 769-5350

**Address**
Central Park West & 79th Street, New York, NY 10024

## The Frick Collection

**Website**
frick.org

**Email**
info@frick.org

**Phone**
(212) 288-0700

**Address**
1 E. 70th Street, New York, NY 10021

## The Metropolitan Museum of Art

**Website**
metmuseum.com/celebrations

**Email**
lisa.doyle@metmuseum.org

**Phone**
Membership Officer for Events and Programs:
Lisa Doyle
(212) 535-7710 or (212) 570-3793

**Address**
1000 Fifth Avenue, New York, NY 10028

## The New Museum

**Website**
newmuseum.org

**Phone**
(212) 219-1222

**Address**
235 Bowery, New York, NY 10002

## The New York Public Library's Stephen A. Schwarzman Building
An iconic landmark building located inside the New York Public Library that has eight exquisite rental spaces.

**Capacity**
Maximum Capacity: 450

**Catering**
Venue provides a list of preferred caterers.

**Website**
nypl.org/spacerental/weddings

**Email**
spev@nypl.org

**Phone**
(212) 930-0730

**Address**
Fifth Avenue at 42nd Street, New York, NY 10018

# UNIVERSITY .............................................................................

## Columbia University Faculty House

**Website**
facultyhouse.columbia.edu

**Email**
fachouse@columbia.edu

**Phone**
(212) 854-1200

**Address**
64 Morningside Drive,
New York, NY 10027

## St. Paul's Chapel at Columbia University
University

**Website**
ouc.columbia.edu/weddings

**Phone**
The Administrative Office
(212) 854-8421

**Address**
1160 Amsterdam Avenue,
New York, NY 10027

## Fordham University Church

**Website**
fordham.edu/info/20111/weddings_at_
fordham

**Email**
weddings@fordham.edu

**Phone**
Office of Campus Ministry at Rose Hill
(718) 817-4518

**Address**
Fordham University Rose Hill Campus,
441 E. Fordham Road, Bronx, NY 10458

# STOCK EXCHANGE ..........................................................

## The New York Stock Exchange

**Website**
nyse.com

**Phone**
(212) 656-2034

**Address**
11 Wall Street, New York, NY 10005

# SKY DIVE .......................................................................

### New York City Skydiving Adventures

**Website**
newyorkskydive.com

**Email**
Contact through website

**Phone**
(855) 445-8973

### Skydiving New York NY

**Website**
skydivingnewyork.com

**Email**
Contact through website

**Phone**
(800) 396-9514

# ZOO .......................................................................

### The Bronx Zoo

**Website**
nyzoosandaquariumevents.com

**Email**
events@wcs.org

**Phone**
(718) 741-3836

**Address**
2300 Southern Boulevard,
Bronx, NY 10460

### The Prospect Park Zoo

**Website**
prospectparkzoo.com

**Email**
events@wcs.org

**Phone**
(718) 741-3836

**Address**
450 Flatbush Avenue,
New York, NY 11225

### The Central Park Zoo

**Website**
centralparkzoo.com

**Email**
events@wcs.org

**Phone**
(718) 741-3836

**Address**
64th Street and Fifth Avenue,
New York, NY 10021

### The Queens Zoo

**Email**
events@wcs.org

**Phone**
(718) 741-3836

**Address**
53-51 111th Street, Corona, NY 11368

# Videographers

## MANHATTAN

### Chris Fig Productions

**Website**
chrisfig.com

**Contact**
Chris Figueroa

**Email**
info@chrisfig.com

**Phone**
(646) 535-6185

**Address**
610 W. 42nd Street, Suite 31E,
New York, NY 10036

### Linda Petrucci Productions

**Website**
lindapetrucci.com

**Contact**
Linda Petrucci

**Email**
info@lindapetrucci.com

**Phone**
(917) 854-5569

**Address**
New York, NY

### Frank Ahn Films

**Website**
frankahnfilms.com/blog

**Contact**
Frank Ahn

**Email**
info@frankahnfilms.com

**Phone**
(347) 239-6403

**Address**
325 W. 38th Street, Suite 1508,
New York, NY 10018

### Marvin Suarez Films

**Website**
marvinsuarezfilms.com

**Contact**
Marvin Suarez

**Email**
info@marvinsuarez.com

**Phone**
(917) 577-8832

**Address**
4876 Broadway, New York, NY 10034

### Hart Pictures

**Website**
hartpictures.com

**Contact**
Founder - Jesse Hart

**Email**
info@hartpictures.com

**Phone**
(212) 791-1651

**Address**
311 E. Broadway, Suite 4,
New York, NY 10002

### Michael Justin Films

**Website**
michaeljustinfilms.com

**Contact**
Michael Justin

**Email**
contact@michaeljustinfilms.com

**Phone**
(914) 487-3077

**Address**
415 E. 84th Street, New York, NY 10028

## Milk & Honey Productions

**Website**
milkandhoneyproductions.com

**Contact**
Zev Greenfield, Owner

**Email**
info@milkandhoneyproductions.com

**Phone**
(212) 725-0014

**Address**
116 W. 23rd Street, Suite 500,
New York, NY 11018

## Monomyth Pictures

**Website**
monomythpictures.com

**Contact**
Michael Severance
michael@monomythpictures.com

Andrei Zakow
andrei@monomythpictures.com

**Email**
info@monomythpictures.com

**Phone**
(212) 802-8430

**Address**
375 Greenwich Street, 5th Floor,
New York, NY 10013

## NST Pictures

**Website**
nstpictures.com

**Contact**
Wedding Sales Assistant
Kerry Sullivan

**Email**
info@nstpictures.com

**Phone**
(855) 642-6531

**Address**
469 Seventh Avenue, 12th Floor,
New York, NY 10018

## Orange Films

**Website**
orangefilmsny.com

**Contact**
Founder and Creative Director
Edward Zilberman
edward@orangefilmsny.com

**Email**
edward@orangefilmsny.com

**Phone**
(800) 859-8797

**Address**
265 Canal Street, Suite 206,
New York, NY 10013

## Roey Yadgar Films

**Website**
ryfilms.com

**Contact**
Founder
Roey Yadgar

**Email**
info@ryfilms.com

**Phone**
(212) 920-6181

**Address**
336 W. 37th Street, Suite 1170,
New York, NY 10018

## The Light Mill

**Website**
thelightmill.com

**Contact**
Geoffrey Boka, Owner

**Email**
boka@thelightmill.com

**Phone**
(800) 729-0414

**Address**
16 W. 38th Street, New York, NY 10016

## Tweed Weddings

**Website**
tweedweddings.com

**Contact**
Raelle Brown
Raelle@tweedvideo.com

**Email**
Contact through website

**Phone**
(267) 318-7032

**Address**
113 E. 31st Street, 4th Floor,
New York, NY 11016

# BROOKLYN

## Hello Super Studios

**Website**
hellosuperstudios.com

**Contact**
Megan Hill, Creative Director

**Email**
info@hellosuperstudios.com

**Phone**
(213) 675-0465

**Address**
208 Washington Park, Suite 3B,
Brooklyn, NY 11205

## Love + Brain Films

**Website**
lovebrainfilms.com

**Contact**
Represented by The Wedding Artist
Collective: Lisa@theweddingac.com

**Email**
Lisa@theweddingac.com

**Phone**
(651) 442-1215

**Address**
486 3rd Street, Brooklyn, NY 11215

## Kiss The Bride Films

**Website**
kissthebridefilms.com

**Email**
kissthebridefilms@gmail.com

**Phone**
(415) 725-6622

**Address**
56 S. 11th Street, Brooklyn, NY 11211

## Shooting Stars Weddings

**Website**
shootingstarsweddings.com

**Contact**
Founder & Principal Photographer
Will Star

**Email**
service@shootingstarsweddings.com

**Phone**
(917) 342-2082

**Address**
374 S. 2nd Street, Suite 7,
Brooklyn, NY  11222

# QUEENS ...........................

## Future Perfect Films

**Website**
futureperfectfilms.com

**Contact**
Rebecca & Mark Landers

**Email**
info@futureperfectfilms.com

**Phone**
(646) 564-3449 or
Toll Free: (888) 499-5657

**Address**
1919 24th Avenue, Astoria, NY 11102

# WESTCHESTER ..................

## Dideo Film Photography

**Website**
dideofilmsphotography.com

**Contact**
Danielle and David Schneider

**Email**
info@dideofilmsphotography.com

**Phone**
(646) 245-0087

**Address**
37 Croton Avenue, Tarrytown, NY 10591

# NEW JERSEY .......................

## Nayeem Vohra Photography and Cinematography (Specializes in South Asian Weddings)

**Website**
nayeemvohra.com

**Contact**
Nayeem Vohra
nayeem@nayeemvohra.com

**Email**
info@nayeemvohra.com

**Phone**
(856) 520-0344

**Address**
Cherry Hill, New Jersey

# ONLINE ..................................

## Pacific Pictures (Specializes in South Asian Weddings)

**Website**
pacificpictures.net

**Email**
info@pacificpictures.net

**Phone**
(714) 839-0020

# Wedding Cakes

## MANHATTAN

### A White Cake

A small custom bakery that specializes in all types of elegant custom cakes, from streamlined and elegant to ornate and fanciful.

**Website**
awhitecake.com

**Contact**
Lauren Bohl White

**Email**
lauren@awhitecake.com

**Phone**
(917) 513-9559

**Address**
335 W. 38th Street, 11th Floor,
New York, NY 10018

### Butterfly Bakeshop

A custom cake shop that provides one-of-a-kind cakes for weddings and special occassions.

**Website**
butterflybakeshop.com

**Contact**
Executive Chef
Orlando Leon

**Email**
contact@butterflybakeshop.com

**Phone**
(212) 686-2253

**Address**
133 E. 39th Street, 2nd Floor,
New York, NY 10016

### Ana Parzych Cakes

A couture wedding cake and specialty cake studio that specializes in one-of-a-kind lavish custom cakes.

**Website**
connecticutweddingcakes.com

**Contact**
Ana Parzych

**Email**
info@anaparzychcakes.com

**Phone**
(212) 390-1667

**Address**
200 W. 57th Street, Suite 307,
New York, NY 10019

### Cake Alchemy

A cake shop that specializes in the science of confectionary design.

**Website**
cakealchemy.com

**Contact**
Owner and Manager
Lauri Ditunno

**Email**
Contact through website

**Phone**
(212) 255-0584

**Address**
336 E. 59th Street, New York, NY 10022

## Cakes By Nicolle

This company specializes in custom design wedding cakes, novelty cakes, and confections. All of its cakes are baked from scratch using high-quality ingredients.

**Website**
cakesbynicolle.com

**Contact**
Nicolle Rodriguez

**Email**
info@cakesbynicolle.com

**Phone**
 (917) 579-0034

**Address**
161 W. 54th Street, New York, NY 10019

## CMNY Cakes

A specialty cakes company that offers wedding cakes and cakes for all occassions.

**Website**
cmnycakes.com

**Contact**
Co-owner
Mona

**Email**
info@cmnycakes.com

**Phone**
(347) 625-6560

**Address**
192 Lexington Avenue, 2nd Floor,
New York, NY  10016

## Empire Cake

This company creates custom designed cakes ranging from traditional tiered wedding cakes to one-of-a-kind creations.

**Website**
empirecake.com

**Email**
info@empirecake.com

**Phone**
(212) 242-5858

**Address**
112 Eighth Avenue, New York, NY 10011

## Me Too Cakes

A specialty cakes company that bakes all cakes from scratch using great ingredients and real fruit purees.

**Website**
metoocakes.com

**Contact**
Owner
Amy Landini Kathuria

**Email**
amy@metoocakes.com

**Phone**
(917) 902-8775

**Address**
New York, NY

## Ron Ben-Israel Cakes

Proclaimed "the Manolo Blahnik of wedding cakes" by the New York Times, Ron Ben-Israel is renowned for his specialty and wedding creations.

**Website**
weddingcakes.com

**Contact**
Ron Ben-Israel

**Email**
Contact through website

**Phone**
(212) 625-3369

**Address**
247 W. 38th Street, 13th Floor,
New York, NY 10018

## Sugar Flower Bake Shop

A cake shop that creates unique special occasion and wedding cakes from local and sustainable ingredients. Its cakes feature realistic-looking flowers hand-made from sugar.

**Website**
sugarflowercakeshop.com
**Contact**
Amy Noelle
**Email**
orders@sugarflowercakeshop.com
**Phone**
(212) 993-6441
**Address**
The Arts Building, 336 W. 37th Street, Suite 950, New York, NY 10018

## Sylvia Weinstock Cakes

A favorite among NYC's social elite, Sylvia Weinstock uses the finest ingredients to create cakes that are delicious works of art.

**Website**
sylviaweinstock.com
**Contact**
Founder and Cake Designer
Sylvia Weinstock
sylvia@swcakes.com
**Email**
Contact through website
**Phone**
(212) 925-6698
**Address**
273 Church Street, Suite 3A, New York, NY 10013

## Sweet Corner Bakeshop

A bakery and cake boutique that specializes in wedding and special occasion cakes. All of its products are hand-crafted and made with the best ingredients available.

**Website**
sweetcorner.com
**Contact**
Cake Designer
Rodolfo Goncalves
**Email**
info@sweetcorner.com
**Phone**
(212) 206-8500
**Address**
535 Hudson Street, New York, NY 10014

## William Greenberg Desserts

A renowned bakery that provides Kosher baked goods. It offers chocolate or vanilla custom designed wedding and special occasion cakes with a multitude of delicious fillings.

**Website**
wmgreenbergdesserts.com
**Email**
Contact through website
**Phone**
(212) 861-1340
**Address**
1100 Madison Avenue, New York, NY 10028

# BROOKLYN ·····························································································

## Bay Ridge Bakery

A top-rated bakery in Brooklyn that specializes in custom and traditional wedding cakes. Each cake is made personally by Pastry Chef and Co-owner, Nick Nikolopoulos.

**Website**
bayridgebakery.com
**Contact**
Nick Nikolopoulos, John Nikolopoulos, or Peggy Nikolopoulos
**Email**
info@bayridgebakery.com
**Phone**
(718) 238-0014
**Address**
7805 Fifth Avenue, Brooklyn, NY 11209

## Made In Heaven Cakes

A family business with over 17 years of experience designing elaborate wedding cakes.

**Website**
madeinheavencakes.com
**Contact**
Victoria Zagami
**Email**
victoria@madeinheavencakes.com
**Phone**
(718) 788-2727
**Address**
530 Third Avenue, Brooklyn, NY 11215

## Betty Bakery

A neighborhood bakeshop operated by two award-winning custom cake bakers, Cheryl Kleinman and Ellen Baumwoll.

**Website**
bettybakery.com
**Contact**
Cheryl Kleinman, Operator and renowned Cake Designer of Cheryl Kleinman Cakes or Ellen Baumwall, Operator and renowned Cake Designer of Bijoux Doux Specialty Cakes
**Email**
info@bettybakery.com
**Phone**
(718) 237-2271
**Address**
448 Atlantic Avenue, Brooklyn, NY 11217

# QUEENS

## Cakeline

This nationally acclaimed baker bakes and designs beautiful, delicious wedding and special occasion cakes.

**Website**
cakeline.com
**Contact**
Cynthia Peithman
**Email**
cakeline@earthlink.net
**Phone**
(718) 634-5063
**Address**
220 Beach 132nd Street,
Queens, NY 11694

## Chic Sugars

A custom cake boutique based in Astoria that creates attractive, stylish, fun, and elegant works of sugar art.

**Website**
chicsugars.com
**Contact**
Owner and Operator
Erika Oldham
**Email**
erika@chicsugars.com
**Phone**
(646) 361-4232
**Address**
Astoria, NY

# NEW JERSEY

## Heather Barranco Dreamcakes

This company specializes in custom specialty cakes and designer wedding cakes for clients in the NY and NJ area.

**Website**
heatherbarranco.com
**Contact**
Heather Barranco
**Email**
info@heatherbarranco.com
**Phone**
(212) 920-9777
**Address**
The Club at Orange Lawn,
305 North Ridgewood Road,
South Orange, NJ 07079

# BRIDAL ATTIRE & GIFT REGISTRY

## Bridal Hair and Makeup

### MANHATTAN

### Amy Klewitz Beauty
A NY-based professional hair and make-up artist recognized for her exceptional work in bridal beauty. She specializes in airbrush and natural application, clip in extensions, and hair pieces. Styles range from clean and natural to edgy and artistic.

**Website**
amyklewitzbeauty.com

**Contact**
Amy Klewitz

**Email**
amyklewitzbeauty@gmail.com

**Phone**
(646) 259-1531

**Address**
New York, NY

### Brides By Benedetti
Courtney Benedetti is an experienced hairstylist who specializes in romantic hair, gorgeous waves, and beautiful up dos.

**Website**
bridesbybenedetti.com

**Contact**
Courtney Benedetti

**Email**
Contact through website

**Phone**
(212) 413-6375

**Address**
New York, NY

### Asia Werner Bridal Artistry
A company that provides hair stylists and makeup artists for weddings.

**Website**
asiawerner.com

**Contact**
Asia Werner

**Email**
Contact through website

**Phone**
(347) 224-6429

**Address**
New York, NY

### Daniela Rodriquez NYC
A team of professional hairstylists and makeup artists that offer on location bridal hair and makeup services.

**Website**
danielarodrigueznyc.com

**Contact**
Daniela Rodriguez

**Email**
danielarodrigueznyc@gmail.com

**Phone**
(718) 772-1871

**Address**
New York, NY

## David Maderich

A freelance makeup artist with over 10 years of experience in bridal hair and makeup. He recommends a consultation with the bride at least 1 month prior to the wedding date.

**Website**
davidmaderich.com/bridal.html

**Contact**
David Maderich

**Email**
davidmaderich@gmail.com

**Phone**
(917) 502-9553

**Address**
New York, NY

## Eva Scrivo

A well-known salon that offers high-quality, elegant hair and makeup services for weddings. It can accommodate both formal and casual styles.

**Website**
evascrivo.com/bridal-services

**Email**
reservations@evascrivo.com

**Phone**
(212) 677-7315

### LOCATIONS

Bond Street
50 Bond Street,
New York, NY 10012

Madison Avenue
903 Madison Avenue,
New York, NY 10021

## Eve Whittington & Co.

A company that specializes in nail and makeup services for weddings. Both on location and in-studio options are available.

**Website**
evewhittington.com

**Contact**
Eve Whittington

**Phone**
(347) 526-1604

**Address**
New York, NY

## Face The Day NY

NY-based beauty experts who provide hair and master airbrush makeup services for weddings and private events.

**Website**
facethedayny.com

**Contact**
Ellen Bodkins, Creative Director & Premiere Makeup Artist

**Email**
info@facethedayny.com

**Phone**
(646) 397-1669

**Address**
Medulla Salon, 36 E. 20th Street,
8th Floor,
New York, NY 10003

## Ivanka Lova Makeup & Hair

A NY-based professional hair and makeup artist specializing in beauty and bridal makeup. The company recommends a consultation 3-4 month prior to the wedding date.

**Website**
ivankalova.com

**Contact**
Ivanka Lova

**Email**
makeup@ivankalova.com

**Phone**
(212) 810-9475

**Address**
New York, NY

## Jennifer Margaret Makeup

A NY-based makeup artist that offers makeup services for the entire bridal party. She offers airbrush makeup to all brides to ensure the most flawless, long-lasting looks.

**Website**
jennifermargaretmakeup.com

**Contact**
Jennifer Margaret

**Email**
jennifermargaretmakeup@gmail.com

**Phone**
(516) 385-0387

**Address**
New York, NY

## Jill Hammelman Hair Design

A studio offering bridal hair and make-up services.

**Website**
jillhammelmanhairdesign.com

**Contact**
Hair
Jill Hammelman
Makeup
Sharon Becker

**Email**
extensionsbyjill@gmail.com

**Phone**
(201) 638-9337

**Address**
67 E. 11th Street, Suite 621,
New York, NY 10003

## MG Hair and Makeup

A beauty company that offers premier, on location hair and makeup services for brides.

**Website**
mghairandmakeup.com

**Contact**
Founder & Director:
Megan Garmers

**Email**
Contact through website

**Phone**
(917) 279-7086

**Address**
New York, NY

## NY Bridal Beauty

A beauty company that offers professional wedding day hair and makeup services for brides on location.

**Website**
nybridalbeauty.com

**Contact**
Amanda Shackleton

**Email**
amandashackleton@yahoo.com

**Phone**
(917) 334-6155

**Address**
88 Lexington Avenue, Suite 2F,
New York, NY 10016

## Once Upon A Bride

A company that offers bridal beauty services, such as updos, half-up styles, down styles, airbrush and traditional makeup, clip ins and seamless hair extensions. It's artists will travel to all 5 boroughs.

**Website**
onceuponabride.net

**Contact**
Principle Artist:
Stacey Weinstein,
(516) 840-5160

**Email**
beauty@ouab.com

**Phone**
(212) 353-2350

**Address**
122 W. 26th Street, 12th Floor,
New York, NY 10001

## War Paint International

War Paint International is an award-wining luxury on-site hair and makeup service in New York City. It takes great pride in providing flawless beauty solutions for brides and entire bridal parties.

**Website**
warpaintinternational.com

**Contact**
Founder & Creative Director
Jessica Mae

**Email**
info@warpaintInternational.com

**Phone**
(917) 740-2896

**Address**
New York, NY

## Tamara New York

A beauty company that provides on location hair styling for weddings. It specializes in classic romantic and current hairstyles.

**Website**
tamaranewyork.com

**Contact**
Tamara Saffioti

**Email**
tamara@tamaranewyork.com

**Phone**
(646) 932-1419

**Address**
New York, NY

## Warren Tricomi

A renowned salon that delivers high-end bridal hair and makeup. In-salon or on location services are available.

**Website**
warrentricomi.com

**Contact**
Bridal Services:
Janine

**Email**
janine@warrentricomi.com

**Phone**
(212) 262-8899

**LOCATIONS**

58th Street
1 W. 58th Street, 2nd Floor,
New York, NY 10019

Madison Avenue
1117 Madison Avenue,
New York, NY 10028

Fifth Avenue
125 Fifth Avenue, 2nd Floor,
New York, NY 10003

# BROOKLYN

## Bespoke Beauty & Bridal

A beauty company that offers a full range of hair and makeup services for weddings, including hair styling, make-up, and eyelash extensions.

**Website**
bespokebeautyandbridal.com

**Contact**
Erin Mayhugh, Hairstyling and Annie Reynor, Makeup

**Email**
bespokebeautybridal@gmail.com

**Phone**
(646) 267-2194 or (917) 685-9743

**Address**
138 Nassau Avenue, Brooklyn, NY 11222

## Jackie Schneider Beauty

A company that offers high-end hair and makeup services for weddings. It accommodates requests for both subtle and dramatic styles.

**Website**
jackieschneiderbeauty.com

**Contact**
Jackie Schneider

**Email**
Contact through website

**Phone**
(914) 420-8067

**Address**
238 Saint Marks Avenue, Brooklyn, NY 11238

# QUEENS

## Sharon Slattery Makeup Artist

A celebrity makeup artist with over 30 years of experience.

**Website**
sharonslatterymakeup.com

**Contact**
Sharon Slattery

**Email**
slatts1919@gmail.com

**Phone**
(917) 686-4828

**Address**
6730 Clyde Street, Forest Hills, NY 11375

# Bridal Jewelry

## MANHATTAN

### A. Fishman & Son Diamonds

A direct importer, cutter, and manufacturer of loose diamonds. It also creates engagement rings and fine diamond jewelry in its own factory.

**Website**
afishman.com

**Email**
josh@afishman.com

**Phone**
(212) 869-0085

**Address**
580 Fifth Avenue, Suite 419,
New York, NY 10036

### Aaron Faber Gallery

A company that specializes in contemporary studio jewelry, new and old classic jewelry, and collectible vintage timepieces.

**Website**
aaronfaber.com

**Email**
info@aaronfaber.com

**Phone**
(212) 586-8411

**Address**
666 Fifth Avenue, New York, NY 10103

### Alexis Bittar

This company offers the latest fashion jewelry for women, including bangles, bracelets, earrings, necklaces, and more.

**Website**
alexisbittar.com

**LOCATIONS**

SoHo
465 Broome Street, NY, NY 10013
**Email**
soho@alexisbittar.com
**Phone**
(212) 727-1093

West Village
353 Bleecker Street, NY, NY 10014
**Email**
bleecker@alexisbittar.com
**Phone**
(212) 727-1093

Madison Avenue
1100 Madison Avenue, NY, NY 10028
**Email**
madison@alexisbittar.com
**Phone**
(212) 249-3649

Columbus Avenue
410 Columbus Avenue, NY, NY 10024
**Email**
columbus@alexisbittar.com
**Phone**
(646) 590-4142

## Alice Kwartler Antiques

A jewelry shop that specializes in antiques, estate jewelry, vintage pieces, signed jewelry, bridal gifts, and silvers.

**Website**
alicekwartler.com

**Email**
alice@alicekwartler.com

**Phone**
(212) 752-3590

**Address**
445 Park Avenue, New York, NY 10022

## Cartier

Makers and sellers of wedding and engagement rings, diamond jewelry, and other luxury goods.

**Website**
cartier.com

**Email**
Contact through website

### LOCATIONS

Fifth Avenue
767 Fifth Avenue, New York, NY 10022
**Phone**
(212) 457-3202

Madison Avenue
828 Madison Avenue,
New York, NY 10021
**Phone**
(212) 472-6400

## David Alan Jewelry

This company has over 20 years of experience providing elegant modern and classic handcrafted jewelry.

**Website**
davidalanjewelry.com

**Email**
info@davidalanjewelry.com

**Phone**
(212) 382-1410

**Address**
2 W. 45th Street, Suite 1403,
New York, NY 10036

## David Levy Diamonds & Fine Jewels, Inc.

A jeweler with over 40 years of experience in all aspects of diamond manufacturing and jewelry design.

**Website**
diamondmatchmaker.com

**Email**
info@diamondmatchmaker.com

**Phone**
(212) 398-8952

**Address**
36 W. 47th Street, Suite 903,
New York, NY 10036

## DVVS Fine Jewelry

A full service jewelry store that specializes in custom design, engagement rings, loose diamonds, and wedding rings.

**Website**
dvvsjewelry.com

**Email**
dvvs@dvvs.com

**Phone**
(212) 366-4888 or (212) 366-4114

**Address**
263 W. 19th Street, New York, NY 10011

## Erica Weiner

A purveyor of affordable vintage-inspired jewelry and antique wedding accessories.

**Website**
ericaweiner.com

**Email**
sales@ericaweiner.com

**Phone**
(212) 334-6383

**Address**
173 Elizabeth Street, New York, NY 10012

## Erstwhile Jewelry
Jewelers that specialize in fine antique pieces dating from the Victorian era to the 40s.

**Website**
erstwhilejewelry.com

**Email**
info@erstwhilejewelry.com

**Phone**
(212) 390-1144

**Address**
589 Fifth Avenue, New York, NY 10017

## Fred Leighton
A renowned jeweler known for its extraordinary vintage style and rare collectible jewels.

**Website**
fredleighton.com

**Email**
Contact through website

**Phone**
(212) 288-1872

**Address**
773 Madison Avenue,
New York, NY 10065

## Greenwich Jewelers
A downtown NYC jewelry boutique with a personally curated selection of fine and fashion jewelry.

**Website**
greenwichjewelers.com

**Email**
info@greenwichjewelers.com

**Phone**
(212) 964-7592

**Address**
64 Trinity Place, New York, NY 10006

## Jelena Behrend Studio
A jeweler specializing in wedding and engagement rings and unique hand forged pieces.

**Website**
jelenabehrendstudio.com

**Email**
info@jelenabehrendstudio.com

**Phone**
(212) 995-8497

**Address**
158 Ludlow Street, New York, NY 10002

## Ken & Dana Design
This jewelry company provides hand-made and custom engagement rings and wedding bands that are locally crafted in NYC.

**Website**
shop.kenanddanadesign.com

**Email**
info@kenanddanadesign.com

**Phone**
(212) 972-7031

**Address**
243 W. 30th Street, 10th Floor,
New York, NY 10001

## Leon Diamond
Located in Manhattan's diamond district on 47th Street, this company offers a high-quality selection of diamond jewlery and superior service.

**Website**
diamondengagementringsnyc.com

**Email**
diamond_avi@yahoo.com

**LOCATIONS**

74 W. 47th Street,
New York, NY 10036
**Phone**
(212) 302-7327

44 West 47th Street, GF-01,
New York, NY 10036
**Phone**
(212) 575-0657

## Lola & Madison

A company that specializes in stylish bridal jewelry and handmade original couture wedding accessories at an affordable price.

**Website**
lolaandmadison.com

**Phone**
(347) 827-8629

**Address**
New York, NY

## Marisa Perry

A jewelry design company that specializes in wedding bands and custom jewelry with elegant designs.

**Website**
marisaperry.com

**Email**
sales@marisaperry.com

**Phone**
(212) 566-8977

**Address**
636 Hudson Street, New York, NY 10014

## Norman Landsberg

A premier NYC jeweler specializing in GIA certified diamonds in any shape, size, or quality.

**Website**
normanlandsberg.com

**Email**
info@normanlandsberg.com

**Phone**
(212) 391-1980

**Address**
66 W. 47th Street, New York, NY 10036

## Regina B. Jewelry

This store features a full line of bridal earrings, bridal bracelets, bridal hair combs, and couture veils.

**Website**
reginab.com

**Email**
info@reginab.com

**Phone**
(917) 721-6805

**Address**
303 Fifth Avenue, New York, NY 10016

## Salvatore & Co.

This company is based in the heart of NYC's world-renowned diamond district on 47th Street.

**Website**
salvatoreandco.com

**Email**
info@salvatoreandco.com

**Phone**
(212) 398-1200

**Address**
55 W. 47th Street, Booth 39,
New York, NY 10036

## The Diamond Co.

One of the nation's leading cutters, importers, designers, and manufacturers of fine jewelry for over 40 years.

**Website**
thediamondco.com

**Email**
info@thediamondco.com

**Phone**
(888) 825-1233 or (212) 819-0336

**Address**
62 W. 47th Street, New York, NY 10036

## Thomas Laine

A luxury jewelry retailer that specializes in bridal jewelry and wedding accessories.

**Website**
thomaslaine.com

**Email**
customerservice@thomaslaine.com

**Phone**
(800) 893-1153 or (646) 688-2361

**Address**
915 Broadway, Suite 903,
New York, NY 10010

## Wedding Ring Originals

This company offers a selection of unique designs for wedding and engagement rings in platinum and gold.

**Website**
weddingrings.com

**Email**
info@weddingrings.com

**Phone**
(800) 522-1175 or (212) 751-3940

**Address**
608 Fifth Avenue, Suite 509,
New York, NY 10020

## Tiffany & Co.

This brand has provided spectacular jewelry and outstanding customer service since 1837.

**Website**
tiffany.com

**Email**
Contact through website

**Customer Service Phone Number**
(800) 843-3269

### LOCATIONS

Fifth Avenue
727 Fifth Avenue, New York, NY 10022
**Phone**
(212) 755-8000

Greene Street
97 Greene Street, New York, NY 10012
**Phone**
(212) 226-6136

Wall Street
37 Wall Street, New York, NY 10005
**Phone**
(212) 514-8015

# BROOKLYN

## Catbird

A Brooklyn-based company that carries a carefully curated selection from exciting jewelry designers. It also carries its in-house line of jewelry.

**Website**
catbirdnyc.com

**Email**
customerservice@catbirdnyc.com or weddings@catbirdnyc.com

**Phone**
(718) 599-3457

### LOCATIONS

Main Store
219 Bedford Avenue, Brooklyn, NY 11211.

Wedding Annex
540 Driggs Avenue, Brooklyn, NY 11211

## Elleven

A fine jewelry boutique that specializes in handmade custom jewelry, including vintage and antique pieces.

**Website**
ellevennyc.com

**Email**
ellevennyc@gmail.com

**Phone**
(718) 624-2611

**Address**
98 Smith Street, Brooklyn, NY 11201

# Bridal Salons

## MANHATTAN

### Adrienne's
A boutique bridal salon that specializes in custom bridal gowns. It also carries outside vendors.

**Website**
adriennesny.com

**Email**
adriennesbridal@gmail.com

**Phone**
(212) 228-9618 or (212) 475-4206

**Address**
134 Orchard Street, New York, NY 10002

### Bridal Garden
The only not-for-profit bridal boutique in NYC. It features donated designer wedding gowns discounted up to 75% off the original retail price.

**Website**
bridalgarden.org

**Email**
staff@bridalgarden.org

**Phone**
(212) 252-0661

**Address**
54 W. 21st Street, Suite 901, New York, NY 10010

### Bergdorf Goodman Bridal Salon
A bridal salon with an extensive collection of beautiful gowns and an elegant, private shopping experience for its clients.

**Website**
bergdorfgoodman.com (search: "bridal")

**Phone**
(212) 872-8957

**Address**
Solow Building, 754 Fifth Avenue, 7th Floor, New York, NY 10019

### Bridal Reflections
A family owned and operated bridal salon that carries a fine selection of couture bridal gowns, veils, headpieces, and accessories. It also provides bridal seamstresses and gown preservation.

**Website**
bridalreflections.com

**Email**
Contact through website

**Phone**
(212) 764-3040

**Address**
260 Fifth Avenue, New York, NY 10001

## Designer Loft

A full-service bridal shop that stocks a wide range of gowns to suit all body types.

**Website**
designerloftnyc.com

**Email**
fashiondesigner@designerloftnyc.com

**Phone**
(212) 944-9013

**Address**
226 W. 37th Street, New York, NY 10018

## Kleinfeld

This shop carries the largest selection of couture wedding dresses, designer exclusives, plus-size wedding gowns, headpieces and accessories.

**Website**
kleinfeldbridal.com

**Email**
Contact through website

**Phone**
General: (646) 633-4300.
For appointments: (646) 633-4365

**Address**
110 W. 20th Street, New York, NY 10011

## Gabriella New York Bridal Salon

An intimate, relaxed bridal boutique that carries an assortment of couture gowns, veils, and headpieces that are unique to the shop.

**Website**
gabriellanewyork.com

**Email**
info@gabriellanewyork.com

**Phone**
(212) 206-1915

**Address**
155 Wooster Street, Suite 3W,
New York, NY 10012

## L'Fay Bridal

An upscale bridal shop that carries European designers and has spacious private fitting rooms.

**Website**
lfay.com

**Email**
nyc@lfay.com

**Phone**
(212) 671-1051

**Address**
215 E. 58th Street, 6th Floor,
New York, NY 10022

## Kelima K

A designer bridal shop that carries custom couture wedding gowns, simple bridal dresses, and wedding attire for indie, vintage, and casual beach brides.

**Website**
kelima.com

**Email**
Contact through website

**Phone**
(212) 334-6546

**Address**
611 Broadway, Suite 538
New York, NY 10012

## Lovely Bride

A chic bridal boutique that carries well-known, indie, and up-and-coming designers.

**Website**
lovelybride.com

**Email**
nyc@lovelybride.com

**Phone**
(212) 924-2050

**Address**
182 Duane Street, Gound Level,
New York, NY 10013

## Mark Ingram Altelier

A premier bridal salon that offers an intimate salon setting and a wide selection of gowns from top of the line bridal and special occasion designers.

**Website**
markingramatelier.com

**Phone**
(212) 319-6778

**Address**
The Park 55 Building,110 E. 55th Street,
8th Floor,
New York, NY 10022

## Pronovias

The NY flagship store for Pronovias Bridal Collection, which carries gowns, veils, headpieces, and accessories.

**Website**
pronovias.us

**Email**
Contact through website

**Phone**
(212) 897-6393

**Address**
14 E. 52nd Street, New York, NY 10022

## Mika Inatome

A bridal salon with over 20 years of experience in providing slim, custom-made bridal gowns.

**Website**
mikainatome.com

**Email**
Contact through website

**Phone**
(212) 966-7777

**Address**
325 W. 38th Street, Suite 407,
New York, NY 10018

## RK Bridal

This shop carries elegant bridal gowns for the entire bridal party at an affordable price.

**Website**
rkbridal.com

**Email**
info@rkbridal.com

**Phone**
(212) 947-1155

**Address**
619 W. 54th Street, 5th Floor,
New York, NY 10019

## Nicole Miller

This bridal selection includes sophisticated, modern styles that are versatile and effortlessly chic.

**Website**
nicolemiller.com/bridal

**Email**
info@nicolemiller.com

**Phone**
(212) 219-1825

**Address**
77 Greene Street, New York, NY 10012

## Saja Wedding

A non-traditional wedding designer that offers delicate, modern wedding gowns at an affordable price.

**Website**
sajawedding.com

**Email**
contact@sajawedding.com

**Phone**
(212) 226-7570

**Address**
368 Broadway, Suite 513,
New York, NY 10013

## Saks Fifth Avenue Bridal Boutique

A bridal salon known for its wide assortment of wedding gowns, outstanding customer service, and knowledgable bridal consultants.

**Website**
saksfifthavenue.com/bridal

**Phone**
(212) 753-4000

**Address**
611 Fifth Avenue, New York, NY 10022

## Selia Yang

A luxury brand that brings modern elegance to bridal fashion.

**Website**
seliayang.com

**Email**
info@seliayang.com

**Phone**
(212) 480-4252

**Address**
15 Broad Street, New York, NY 10005

## Shareen Vintage

A collection of elegant white gowns for the non-traditional bride. The store also carries a curated selection of pristine vintage bridal dresses.

**Website**
shareen.com

**Email**
contactny@shareen.com or bridal@shareen.com

**Phone**
(212) 206-1644

**Address**
13 W. 17th Street, New York, NY 10011

## Stone Fox Bride

An alternative, relaxed wedding showroom that carries a curated selection of bridal gowns, veils, headpieces and rings.

**Website**
stonefoxbride.com

**Email**
info@stonefoxbride.com

**Phone**
(212) 260-8600

**Address**
611 Broadway, Suite 613B, New York, NY 10012

## The White Gown

A full-service bridal boutique that offers alterations, gown cleaning, preservation, and bridal appointments with a personal consultant.

**Website**
thewhitegown.com

**Email**
info@thewhitegown.com

**Phone**
(212) 922-9310

**Address**
3 E. 44th Street, 5th Floor, New York, NY 10017

# BROOKLYN

## Bridal Styles Boutique

A premier NY bridal accessory show-room that features top national and international couture designers. It also carries private designers that are exclusive to the boutique.

**Website**
BridalStylesBoutique.com

**Email**
info@bridalstylesboutique.com

**Phone**
(718) 339-3222

**Address**
905 Avenue U, Brooklyn, NY 11223

## VeKa Bridal

An intimate bridal boutique featuring innovative, indie designers that challenge the traditional view of the bridal industry.

**Website**
vekabridal.com

**Email**
info@vekabridal.com

**Phone**
(718) 222-1178

**Address**
412 Atlantic Avenue, Brooklyn, NY 11201

## Isabella's Wedding Center

A bridal salon with over 14 years of experiencing dressing brides and their bridal parties.

**Website**
isabellasweddingcenter.com

**Email**
info@weddingretailer.com

**Phone**
(877) 694-6967

**Address**
2299 Coney Island Avenue, Brooklyn, NY 11223

# Bridal Veil and Headpieces

## MANHATTAN

### Basia Custom Headdress and Accessories

This store offers high-end handmade headpieces and veils embroidered with ribbons, pearls, feathers, and Swarovski crystals.

**Phone**
(212) 874-6720

**Address**
304 Columbus Avenue,
New York, NY 10023

### Bridal Reflections

A family owned and operated bridal salon that carries a fine selection of couture bridal gowns, veils, headpieces, and accessories.

**Website**
bridalreflections.com

**Email**
Contact through website

**Phone**
(212) 764-3040

**Address**
260 Fifth Avenue, New York, NY 10001

### Ellen Christine Millinery

This shop carries a bridal line of millinery couture headwear and veils.

**Website**
ellenchristinecouture.com

**Email**
Contact through website

**Phone**
(212) 242-2457

**Address**
99 Vandam Street, New York, NY 10013

### Gabriella New York Bridal Salon

An intimate, relaxed bridal boutique that carries an assortment of couture gowns, veils, and headpieces that are unique to the shop.

**Website**
gabriellanewyork.com

**Email**
info@gabriellanewyork.com

**Phone**
(212) 206-1915

**Address**
155 Wooster Street, Suite 3W,
New York, NY 10012

### Kleinfeld

This shop carries the largest selection of couture wedding dresses, designer exclusives, plus-size wedding gowns, headpieces and accessories.

**Website**
kleinfeldbridal.com

**Email**
Contact through website

**Phone**
General: (646) 633-4300.
For appointments: (646) 633-4365

**Address**
110 W. 20th Street, New York, NY 10011

## M&J Bridal Salon

A bridal salon that specializes in veils, headpieces and accessories.

**Website**
mjbridalsalon.com

**Email**
bridal@mjtrim.com

**Phone**
(212) 704-8017

**Address**
1008 Avenue of the Americas, New York, NY 10018

## Regina B. Jewelry

This store features a full line of bridal earrings, bridal bracelets, bridal hair combs, and couture veils.

**Website**
reginab.com

**Email**
info@reginab.com

**Phone**
(917) 721-6805

**Address**
303 Fifth Avenue, New York, NY 10016

## Pronovias

The NY flagship store for Pronovias Bridal Collection, which carries gowns, veils, headpieces, and accessories.

**Website**
pronovias.us

**Email**
Contact through website

**Phone**
(212) 897-6393

**Address**
14 E. 52nd Street, New York, NY 10022

## Sposabella Lace

A shop that specializes in wedding veils, tiaras, and embellishments. It offers a variety of lace styles to meet the needs of any bride.

**Website**
sposabellanyc.com

**Email**
sposabellalace@aol.com

**Phone**
(212) 354-4729

**Address**
240 W. 37th Street, New York, NY 10018

# Bridesmaid Dresses

## MANHATTAN

### Bella Bridesmaids
A store that carries a large collection of custom designer bridesmaids dresses.

**Website**
bellabridesmaids.com

**Email**
nyc@bellabridesmaids.com

**Phone**
(212) 695-2700

**Address**
545 Eighth Avenue,
Suite 1525,
New York, NY 10018

### Designer Loft
This shop carries bridesmaids dresses, mother-of-the-bride dresses, flowergirl dresses, and bridal accessories for all.

**Website**
designerloftnyc.com

**Address**
226 W. 37th Street, 2nd Floor,
New York, NY 10018

**Email**
fashion@designerloftnyc.com

**Phone**
(212) 944-9013

### Claudia Hanlin's Wedding Library
The flagship store for bridesmaid designers Amsale, Milly, and Coren Moore. It carries the broadest selection of bridesmaids dresses in New York.

**Website**
theweddinglibrary.com/bridesmaids

**Email**
ido@theweddinglibrary.com

**Phone**
(212) 327-0100

**Address**
14 E. 60th Street, Suite 606,
New York, NY 10022

### Here Comes the Bridesmaid
An elegant bridesmaids dress salon located in the center of NYC.

**Website**
bridesmaids.com

**Email**
info@bridesmaids.com

**Phone**
(212) 647-9686

**Address**
213 W. 35th Street, Suite 403,
New York, NY

# Gift Registry

## MANHATTAN

### ABC Carpet & Home
This celebrated store offers a hand-cu-rated assortment of rugs, furniture, antiques, textiles and accessories from around the world.

**Website**
abchome.com

**Email**
homeregistry@abchome.com

**Phone**
(646) 602-3731

**Address**
888 & 881 Broadway,
New York, NY 10003

### Baccaret
An iconic brand that specializes in fine crystal jewelry, lighting, bar and table-ware, and gifts for special occasions.

**Website**
us.baccarat.com

**Contact**
Customer Service
(800) 215-1300
baccarat.customerservice@baccarat.com

Store:
(212) 826-4100
madison_ave.store@baccarat.fr

**Address**
635 Madison Avenue,
New York, NY 10022

### Alessi
One of the leading factories of Italian design that offers high-quality products.

**Website**
alessi.com

**Email**
retail.soho@alessi.com

**Phone**
(212) 941-7300

**Address**
130 Greene Street, New York, NY 10012

### Bloomingdale's
The Registry offers household items for dining and entertainment, bed and bath, kitchen, home decor, luggage, cleaning, and organization.

**Website**
bloomingdales.com

**Phone**
Registry
(212) 705-3340
Store
(212) 705-2000

**Address**
1000 Third Avenue, New York, NY 10022

## Broadway Panhandler

One of the first gourmet cooking stores in NYC offering high-quality specialty cookware, knives, bakeware, kitchen tools, tabletop accessories, and more.

**Website**
broadwaypanhandler.com

**Email**
bpisales@broadwaypanhandler.com

**Phone**
(866) 266-5927 or (212) 966-3434

**Address**
65 E. 8th Street, New York, NY 10003

## Crate & Barrel

An affordable modern furnishings store that offers furniture, tableware, kitchenware, home accessories, and décor that are inspired by iconic designs.

**Website**
crateandbarrel.com

**Email**
Contact through website

**Phone**
(212) 780-0004

**Address**
611 Broadway, New York, NY 10012

## Frette

An Italian textile company that produces linens and home furnishings of unparalleled quality.

**Website**
frette.com

**Email**
info@frette.com

**Phone**
(212) 988-5221

**Address**
800 Madison Avenue,
New York, NY 10065

## Global Table

A table-top and home accessories store that stocks a carefully edited selection of dishes, glassware, and accessories from around the world.

**Website**
globaltable.com

**Email**
nathalie@globaltable.com

**Phone**
(212) 431-5839

**Address**
107 Sullivan Street, New York, NY 10012

## Sur La Table

This store offers a selection of exclusive premium-quality cookware, dinnerware, kitchen electrics, bakeware, and more.

**Website**
surlatable.com

**LOCATIONS**
Upper East Side
1320 Third Avenue,
New York, NY 10021

**Phone**
(646) 843-7984

**Email**
slt084@surlatable.com

Midtown
306 W. 57th Street,
New York, NY 10019

**Phone**
(212) 574-8334

**Email**
slt102@surlatable.com

SoHo
75 Spring Street,
New York, NY 10012

**Phone**
(212) 966-3375

**Email**
slt052@surlatable.com

## The Future Perfect

This store features new design furnishings locally made in an online boutique setting.

**Website**
thefutureperfect.com

**Email**
perfect@thefutureperfect.com

**Phone**
(877) 388-7373 or (212) 473-2500

**Address**
55 Great Jones Street,
New York, NY 10012

# BROOKLYN

## A & G Merch

A Brooklyn-based home furnishings store that supplies unique, quality, affordable items.

**Website**
aandgmerch.com

**Email**
wburg@aandgmerch.com

**Phone**
(718) 388-1779

**Address**
111 N. 6th Street, Brooklyn,
New York 11249

## The Brooklyn Kitchen

A kitchen store that offers quality tools and equipment, ingredient-driven groceries, and technique-based recreational cooking classes.

**Website**
thebrooklynkitchen.com

**Email**
orders@thebrooklynkitchen.com

**Phone**
(718) 389-2982

**Address**
100 Frost Street, Brooklyn,
New York 11211

## Whisk

A store owned and run by Brooklyn locals who stock a full range of kitchenware and tabletop items.

**Website**
whisknyc.com

**Email**
info@whisknyc.com

### LOCATIONS

Manhattan
933 Broadway, New York, NY 10010

**Phone**
(212) 477-8680

Brooklyn
231 Bedford Avenue, Brooklyn, NY 11211

**Phone**
(718) 218-7230

# ONLINE

### Better Ever After

Instead of wedding registry gifts, this company offers fun, exciting activities that couples can experience together. Activities include wine tastings, sky diving, art classes, and unique get-aways.

**Website**
bettereverafter.com

**Email**
hello@bettereverafter.com

### Honeyfund

The leading online wedding gift registry that makes it easy to give and receive the perfect wedding gift.

**Website**
honeyfund.com

**Email**
Contact through website

### CityBird

A gifting platform registry for experiences, date nights, and activities in NYC.

**Website**
citybirdregistry.com

**Email**
hello@citybirdregistry.com

### Zola

An all-in-one wedding registry for the always-online, on-the-go couple. The company is transforming how couples and guests share, buy, and ship wedding gifts.

**Website**
zola.com

**Email**
support@zola.com

# Seamstress and Tailor

## MANHATTAN

### Alterations Master Tailor Shop

A family owned and operated company with experienced, skilled, and professionally trained tailors that understand how garments should fit the body. It specializes in men's tailoring, women's tailoring, custom suits, and custom shirts.

**Website**
alterationsmaster.com

**Contact**
Head Seamstress at Women's Location
Grace
Head Tailor Men's Location
JD

**Email**
email@alterationsmaster.com

**LOCATIONS**
Men's Location
545 Fifth Avenue,
8th Floor,
New York, NY 10017

**Phone**
(212) 655-9679

Women's Location
590 Madison Avenue,
21st Floor,
New York, NY 10022

**Phone**
(212) 845-9913

### Ann Hamilton Bridal

A tailor company that specializes in vintage restoration, alteration, and redesign. It also offers contemporary bridal alterations and veils.

**Website**
annhamiltonbridal.com

**Contact**
Ann Hamilton

**Email**
annhamiltonbridal@gmail.com

**Phone**
(212) 625-8622

**Address**
463 West Street, New York, NY 10014

### Beyond Bespoke

An award-winning company that combines modern style with classic tailoring to deliver timeless luxury.

**Website**
beyondbespoke.com or
beyondbespoke.com/#beyondbridal

**Contact**
Nick Torres

**Email**
beyondspoke@gmail.com

**Phone**
(212) 918-1966

**Address**
45 W. 46th Street, 2nd Floor,
New York, NY 10036

## Dynasty Custom Tailors

A specialist in garment development for all categories of apparel, including wedding gowns.

**Website**
dynastycustomtailor.com

**Contact**
Joseph Ting

**Email**
infor@dynastytailor.com

**Phone**
(212) 679-1075

**Address**
6 E. 38th Street, New York, NY 10016

## Ghost Tailor

A NYC-based tailor that provides bridal gowns for women and tailoring for all. At-home fittings are available.

**Website**
ghosttailor.com

**Contact**
Jean Kormos, Designer and Owner

**Email**
ghosttailor@earthlink.net

**Phone**
(212) 253-9727

**Address**
153 W. 27th Street, Suite 1100, New York, NY 10001

## Ellen's Couture

A tailor company that specializes exclusively in bridal apparel. It incorporates material of the finest quality to create wedding gowns, bridesmaid dresses, and flower girl dresses.

**Website**
ellenscouture.com

**Contact**
Ellen Canali

**Email**
ellencanali@ellenscouture.com

**Phone**
(212) 496-8800

**Address**
445 Columbus Avenue, New York, NY 10024

## Guillermo Couture

This company has been creating custom-designed bridal dresses, gowns, and formalwear for over two decades.

**Website**
guillermocouture.com

**Contact**
Guillermo Molina

**Email**
guillermo@guillermocouture.com

**Phone**
(212) 366-6965

**Address**
237 W. 37th Street, 13th Floor, New York, NY 10018

## Madame Paulette

A company that provides cleaning, preservation, and professional alterations from highly skilled tailors. Its specialties include restoration of vintage and couture garments, European tailoring, hand laundering of delicate fabrics, and intricate beading.

**Website**
madamepaulette.com

**Contact**
Garment Services Manager
Christine O'Donnell
christine@madamepaulette.com

Corporate Client Services Manager &
Bridal Restoration
Karen
karen@madamepaulette.com

**Email**
asktheexpert@madamepaulette.com

**Phone**
(347) 689-7010

**Address**
1255 Second Avenue,
New York, NY 10065

## Selene Alterations & Custom Designs

A company with over 30 years of experience providing high-end alterations for bridal gowns, vintage dresses, womenswear, and menswear.

**Website**
selenenyc.com

**Contact**
Selene

**Email**
info@selenenyc.com

**Phone**
(212) 777-1908

**Address**
271 E. 10th Street, New York, NY 10009

## Sew Elegant

This company, which is known for its exquisite tailoring skills and ability to re-create designer dresses, specializes in high-end alterations, custom made and vintage wedding gowns, and veils.

**Website**
sewelegantny.com/services

**Contact**
Esin Kirmizidag

**Phone**
(212) 764-1701

**Address**
108 W. 39th Street, Suite 903,
New York, NY 10018

## Wilfred's Tailor

A team of 8 experienced tailors who each specialize in a particular type of clothing. From simple adjustments to made-to-measure alterations, all tasks are accomplished in-house to guarantee the best quality.

**Website**
wilfredstailor.com

**Email**
wilfredstailor@aol.com

**Phone**
(212) 242-3030

**Address**
277 Fifth Avenue, 3rd Floor,
New York, NY 10016

# BROOKLYN

### The Wedding Dresser
This company offers alterations and restyling with in-home fittings, vintage-inspired accessories, expert tailoring, custom gowns and jackets, refurbished and restyled vintage gowns, bridal attendants for the wedding day, and green dry cleaning and preservation.

**Website**
theweddingdresser.com

**Contact**
Founder
Susan Ruddie
susan@theweddingdresser.com

**Phone**
(347) 743-8493

**Address**
45 Linden Boulevard, Suite 4E,
Brooklyn, New York 11226

# BRONX

### B & B Tailor
A tailor company located in the Bronx, New York.

**Phone**
(718) 655-0117

**Address**
2748 Matthews Avenue, Bronx, NY 10467

### Best Tailors
A tailor company that specializes in custom clothing and apparel. It offers tailoring for both men and women.

**Contact**
Jenny Sim

**Phone**
(718) 549-9017

**Address**
3530 Henry Hudson Parkway,
Bronx, NY 10463

# Tuxedo and Suit

## MANHATTAN

### Alan David Custom
A NYC-based custom tailor specializing in custom suits for men.

**Website**
alandavid.com

**Email**
Contact through website

**Phone**
(888) 850-6716

**Address**
16 E. 40th Street, New York, NY 10016

### Ascot Chang
A company that specializes in individual bespoke dress shirts, suits, and mens-wear.

**Website**
ascotchang.com

**Email**
ny@ascotchang.com

**Phone**
(212) 759-3333

**Address**
110 Central Park South,
New York, NY 10019

### Baldwin Formals
A top-rated NYC tuxedo rental company.

**Website**
nyctuxedos.com

**Email**
info@nyctuxedos.com

**Phone**
(212) 245-8190

**Address**
1156 Avenue of the Americas,
2nd Floor,
New York, NY 10036

### Beckenstein Bespoke
A company that has earned a reputation as one of the top bespoke suit makers in NYC.

**Website**
fabricczar.com/beckenstein-bespoke.
html

**Email**
steven@beckenstein.com

**Phone**
(212) 475-6666

**Address**
257 W. 39th Street, New York, NY 10018

### Brioni
An exclusive brand of tailored clothing that provides made-to-measure services and sportswear for men.

**Website**
brioni.com

**Email**
info@brioni.com

**LOCATIONS**
52nd Street
55 E. 52nd Street, Suite 7,
New York, NY 10055

**Phone**
(212) 355-1940

57th Street
57 E. 57th Street, New York, NY 10022

**Phone**
(212) 376-5777

### Cesare Attolini

This clothing company offers bespoke suits for refined men.

**Website**
cesareattolini.com

**Email**
info@cesareattolini.com

**Phone**
(646) 707-3006

**Address**
798 Madison Avenue,
New York, NY 10065

### Duncan Quinn

A company that specializes in luxury slim-fitted suits, with both off-the-rack and custom options available. It also offers unique ties and accessories.

**Website**
duncanquinn.com

**Email**
help@duncanquinn.com

**Phone**
(212) 226-7030

**Address**
70 Kenmare Street, New York, NY 10012

### Charles Tyrwhitt

A company that produces fine menswear with timeless style and uncompromising quality.

**Website**
ctshirts.com

**Email**
madisonavenue.shop@ctshirts.co.uk

**Phone**
(212) 286-8988

**Address**
377 Madison Avenue,
New York, NY 10017

### Freemans Sporting Club

A men's retailer that specializes in custom suits and handmade goods.

**Website**
freemanssportingclub.com

**Email**
Info@Freemanssportingclub.com

**Phone**
(212) 673-3209

**Address**
8 Rivington Street, New York, NY 10002

### Doyle Mueser

A NYC shop that specializes in slim-fitting men's suits and elevated menswear.

**Website**
doylemueser.com

**Email**
info@doylemueser.com

**Phone**
(347) 982-4382

**Address**
19 Christopher Street,
New York, NY 10014

### Hickey Freeman

A company that specializes in luxury tailored clothing for men.

**Website**
hickeyfreeman.com

**Email**
customerservice@hickeyfreeman.com

**Phone**
(212) 586-6481

**Address**
543 Madison Avenue,
New York, NY 10022

## J. Hilburn

A custom clothier for men that creates personalized, made-to-measure suits.

**Website**
jhilburn.com

**Email**
rachel.mohwinkel@jhilburnpartner.com

**Phone**
(866) 789-5381

**Address**
16 W. 23rd Street, New York, NY 10010

## Rothman's NY

A men's clothing company that offers custom and made-to-measure options and on-site tailoring.

**Website**
rothmansny.com

**Email**
Shae@rothmansny.com

**Phone**
(914) 713-0300

**Address**
222 Park Avenue South,
New York, NY 10003

## LS Men's Clothing

A custom tailor that provides high-quality mens bespoke suits at affordable prices. Its custom suits are made in America by custom tailors using old world techniques.

**Website**
lsmensclothing.com

**Email**
lsmens@aol.com

**Phone**
(212) 575-0933

**Address**
49 W. 45th Street, 3rd Floor,
New York, NY 10036

## Saint Laurie Merchant Tailors

A company with over 100 years of experience creating custom suits. It also provides custom tails, morning suits, and custom shirts.

**Website**
saintlaurie.com

**Email**
tailor@saintlaurie.com

**Phone**
(212) 643-1916

**Address**
22 W. 32nd Street, 5th Floor,
New York, NY 10001

# BROOKLYN

### Bindle and Keep
A Brooklyn-based premier bespoke clothing company that uses the finest fabrics.

**Website**
bindleandkeep.com

**Email**
info@bindleandkeep.com

**Phone**
(917) 740-5002

**Address**
Brooklyn, NY 11205

### Gentry
A one stop shop for the best men's brands.

**Website**
gentrynyc.com

**Email**
info@gentrynyc.com

**Phone**
(718) 384-8585

**Address**
108 N. 7th Street,
Suite 101,
Brooklyn, NY 11249

### Brooklyn Tailors
A clothing company that specializes in bespoke and ready to wear suits, shirts, and more.

**Website**
brooklyn-tailors.com

**Email**
custom@brooklyn-tailors.com

**Phone**
(347) 799-1646

**Address**
358 Grand Street, Brooklyn, NY 11211

# LEGAL & CEREMONY

## House of Worship

## MANHATTAN

### All Souls Christian Church
Non-Denominational

On-site officiator

**Website**
allsoulschristianchurch.com

**Email**
life@allsoulschristianchurch.com or
info@apostlesnyc.com

**Phone**
(646) 872-9048

**Address**
265 W. 79th Street, New York, NY 10024

### Archdiocesan Cathedral of the Holy Trinity
Greek Orthodox

**Website**
thecathedral.goarch.org

**Email**
info@thecathedralnyc.org

**Phone**
(212) 288-3215

**Address**
337 E. 74th Street, New York, NY 10021

### Annunciation Greek Orthodox Church
Greek Orthodox

**Website**
annunciation-nyc.org

**Email**
info@annunciation-nyc.org

**Phone**
(212) 724-2070

**Address**
302 W. 91st Street, New York, NY 10024

### Harlem Grace Tabernacle
Non-Denominational

**Website**
harlemgrace.org

**Email**
info@harlemgrace.org

**Phone**
(212) 368-7977

**Address**
256 W. 145th Street, New York, NY 10039

## Islamic Cultural Center of New York
Muslim

On-site officiator

**Website**
icc-ny.us

**Phone**
(212) 722-5234

**Address**
1711 Third Avenue, New York, NY 10029

## Korean Methodist Church and Institute
Christian

Primarily a Korean and Asian-American church that follows the doctrinal standards stated in the Book of Discipline of the United Methodist Church.

**Website**
morningside-nyc.com

**Email**
office@morningside-nyc.com

**Phone**
(212) 662-1422

**Address**
633 W. 115th Street, New York, NY 10025

## Neighborhood Church of Greenwich Village
Presbyterian

On-site officiator

**Website**
ncgv.net

**Email**
ncgv@ncgv.net

**Phone**
(212) 691-1770

**Address**
269 Bleecker Street, New York, NY 10014

## NY Chinese Alliance Church
Non-Denominational

On-site officiator

**Website**
nycac.org

**Phone**
(212) 533-3808

**Address**
162 Eldridge Street, New York, NY 10002

## St. Andrew's Catholic Church
Catholic

**Email**
churchofsaintandrewnyc@verizon.net

**Phone**
(212) 962-3972

**Address**
20 Cardinal Hayes Place,
New York, NY 10007

## St. Barbara Greek Orthodox Church
Greek Orthodox

**Website**
stbarbaragoc.com

**Email**
stbarbaranyc@aol.com

**Phone**
(212) 226-0499

**Address**
27 Forsyth Street, New York, NY 10002

## St. George Greek Orthodox Church
Greek Orthodox

**Website**
saintgeorgenyc.org

**Contact**
Friar Jim

**Email**
frjimk@goarch.org

**Phone**
(212) 265-7808

**Address**
307 W. 54th Street, New York, NY 10019

## St. James Presbyterian Church
Christian

For on-site ceremonies, must be members of the parish or in the process of establishing membership.

**Website**
nycago.org/Organs/NYC/html/StJamesPres.html

**Contact**
Grace Beacham

**Email**
stjames@verizon.net

**Phone**
(212) 283-4541

**Address**
409 W. 141st Street, New York, NY 10031

## St. John the Baptist Greek Orthodox Church
Greek Orthodox

**Website**
stjohn.ny.goarch.org

**Email**
saint.john2011@gmail.com

**Phone**
(212) 473-0648

**Address**
143 E. 17th Street, New York, NY 10003

## St. Stephen of Hungary Parish
Catholic

Marriage arrangements must be made six months in advance.

**Website**
ssh-nyc.org

**Email**
parish@ssh-nyc.org

**Phone**
(212) 861-8500

**Address**
414 E. 82nd Street, New York, NY 10028

## Stephen Wise Free Synagogue
Jewish

Must be a member of synagogue. No interfaith services allowed.

**Website**
swfs.org

**Email**
info@swfs.org

**Phone**
(212) 877-4050

**Address**
30 West 68th Street New York, NY 10023

## The Church of Jesus Christ of Latter-Day Saints
Mormon

On-site officiator

**Website**
https://www.lds.org/church/temples/manhattan-new-york?lang=eng

**Email**
manha-prs@ldschurch.org or manha-rec@ldschurch.org

**Phone**
(917) 441-8220

**Address**
125 Columbus Avenue, New York, NY 10023

## The Church of the Intercession
Episcopalian

Must comply with marriage policies from the Diocese of New York.

**Website**
intercessionnyc.org

**Email**
intercession550@gmail.com

**Phone**
(212) 283-6200

**Address**
550 West 155th Street, New York, NY 10032

## The Riverside Church
Christian

Accepts interfaith, heterosexual and same-sex couples.

**Website**
theriversidechurchny.org

**Contact**
Wedding Coordinator
Angela Gregory

**Email**
Contact through website

**Phone**
(212) 870-6700 or (212) 870-6762

**Address**
490 Riverside Drive, Suite 605T,
New York, NY 10027

## Trinity Church
Catholic

Welcomes interfaith marriages.

**Website**
trinitywallstreet.org

**Email**
contact@trinitywallstreet.org

**Phone**
(212) 602-0800

**Address**
75 Broadway, New York, NY 10006

# BROOKLYN

## East Midwood Jewish Center
Jewish

Offers wedding facilities and kosher catering.

**Website**
emjc.org

**Email**
info@emjc.org

**Phone**
(718) 338-3800

**Address**
1625 Ocean Avenue, Brooklyn, NY 11230

## Ebenezer Wesleyan Methodist Church
Christian

On-site officiator

**Website**
ebenezerwmc.org

**Email**
info@ebenezerwmc.org

**Phone**
(718) 467-3624

**Address**
1024 Bergen Street, Brooklyn, NY 11216

## First Unitarian Congregational Society in Brooklyn
Christian

On-site officiator

**Website**
fuub.org/home

**Contact**
Ceremonies Coordinator
Nicole Tuszynski
nicole@fuub.org

**Email**
garnett@fuub.org

**Phone**
(718) 624-5466

**Address**
116 Pierrepont Street, Brooklyn, NY 11201

# Matrimonial Lawyers

## MANHATTAN ...........................................................................

### Aronson Mayefsky & Sloan

**Website**
amsllp.com

**Email**
inquiries@amsllp.com

**Phone**
(212) 521-3500

**Address**
12 E. 49th Street, New York, NY 10017

### Berkman Bottger Newman & Rodd, LLP

**Website**
berkbot.com

**Email**
Contact through website

**Phone**
(212) 867-9123

**Address**
521 Fifth Avenue, New York, NY 10175

### Blank Rome, LLP

**Website**
blankrome.com

**Email**
Contact through website

**Phone**
(212) 885-5000

**Address**
405 Lexington Avenue,
New York, NY 10174

### Bryant & Bleier, LLP

**Website**
matrimoniallawnewyork.com

**Email**
info@bbdivorce.com

**Phone**
(646) 421-6505

**Address**
305 Broadway, Suite 1400,
New York, NY 10007

### David Centeno Law

**Website**
nyuncontesteddivorceattorney.com

**Email**
Contact through website

**Phone**
(866) 830-2064

**LOCATIONS**
Cortlandt Street
22 Cortlandt Street, 16th Floor,
New York, NY 10007

Broadway
140 Broadway, 46th Floor,
New York, NY 10005

### Kelley Drye & Warren, LLP

**Website**
kelleydrye.com

**Email**
Contact through website

**Phone**
(212) 808-7965

**Address**
101 Park Avenue, New York, NY 10178

## Mayerson, Abramowitz, & Kahn, LLP

**Website**
mak-law.com

**Email**
Contact through website

**Phone**
(212) 685-7474

**Address**
275 Madison Avenue, Suite 1300,
New York, NY 10016

## Miller Zeiderman & Wiederkehr, LLP

**Website**
mzwnylaw.com

**Email**
info@mzw-law.com

**Phone**
(212) 324-3707

**Address**
110 E. 59th Street, 23rd Floor,
New York, NY 10022

## Orenstein & Orenstein, LLC

**Website**
orensteinlaw.com

**Email**
mail@orensteinlaw.com

**Phone**
(212) 754-6300

**Address**
425 Park Avenue, 27th Floor,
New York, NY 10022

## Scott I. Orgel

**Website**
orgellaw.com

**Email**
scott@orgellaw.com

**Phone**
(347) 259-6961

**Address**
445 Park Avenue, 9th Floor,
New York, NY 10022

## Sherri Donovan and Associates, LLP

**Website**
sherridonovan.com

**Email**
sherri@sherridonovan.com

**Phone**
(917) 723-1163 or (212) 431-9076

**Address**
7 Dey Street,
Suite 400,
New York, NY 10007

## The Mandel Law Firm

**Website**
mandellawfirm.com

**Email**
Contact through website

**Phone**
(888) 294-6669 or (212) 697-7383

**Address**
370 Lexington Avenue, Suite 505,
New York, NY 10017

## Wachtel Missry, LLP

**Website**
wmllp.com

**Email**
Contact through website

**Phone**
(866) 526-2877

**Address**
1 Dag Hammarskjold Plaza,
885 Second Avenue,
New York, NY 10017

# BROOKLYN

## Caruso Caruso & Branda Pc

**Website**
carusocarusobranda.com

**Email**
mcaruso@carusobranda.com

**Phone**
(718) 680-5778

**Address**
7302 13th Avenue, Brooklyn, NY 11228

## Lubov Stark

**Website**
lubovstark.com

**LOCATIONS**
Brooklyn
1022 Avenue P, Brooklyn, NY 11223

**Phone**
(718) 998-3600

Manhattan
113 E. 64th Street,
2nd Floor,
New York, NY 10065

**Phone**
(212) 988-6800

## Richard A. Klass, Esq.

**Website**
courtstreetlaw.com

**Email**
richklass@courtstreetlaw.com

**Phone**
(718) 643-6063

**Address**
16 Court Street,
28th Floor,
Brooklyn, NY 11241

# NYC Administration & Useful Numbers

## MANHATTAN

### Department of Parks & Recreations
Parks, Recreation

**Website**
nycgovparks.org

**Phone**
For calls within the 5 boroughs
311
For calls outside the 5 boroughs
(212) 639-9675 or (212) 504-4115

**Address**
24 W. 61st Street, New York, NY 10023

### Office of the City Clerk
Marriage License, Ceremony

**Website**
cityclerk.nyc.gov

**Phone**
For calls within the 5 boroughs
311
For calls outside the 5 boroughs:
(212) 639-9675

**Address**
141 Worth Street, New York, NY 10013

### New York City Hall
Marriage License, Ceremony

**Website**
nyc.gov

**Phone**
(212) 639-9675

**Address**
City Hall Park, New York, NY 10017

### Traffic Ticket Dispute
Parking Tickets

**Website**
nyc.gov/disputeticket

**Phone**
For calls within the 5 boroughs
311
For calls outside the 5 boroughs
(212) 639-9675

# BROOKLYN....................................

## Office of the City Clerk
Marriage License, Ceremony

**Website**
cityclerk.nyc.gov

**Phone**
For calls within the 5 boroughs
311
For calls outside the 5 boroughs
(212) 639-9675

**Address**
Brooklyn Municipal Building
210 Joralemon Street, Room 205,
Brooklyn, NY 11201

# QUEENS....................................

## Office of the City Clerk
Marriage License, Ceremony

**Website**
cityclerk.nyc.gov

**Phone**
For calls within the 5 boroughs
311
For calls outside the 5 boroughs
(212) 639-9675

**Address**
Borough Hall Building
120-55 Queens Boulevard, Ground Floor,
Room G-100, Kew Gardens, NY 11424

# BRONX ....................................

## Office of the City Clerk
Marriage License, Ceremony

**Website**
cityclerk.nyc.gov

**Phone**
For calls within the 5 boroughs: 311
For calls outside the 5 boroughs:
(212) 639-9675

**Address**
Supreme Court Building
851 Grand Concourse, Room B131,
Bronx, NY 10451

# STATEN ISLAND....................

## Office of the City Clerk
Marriage License, Ceremony

**Website**
cityclerk.nyc.gov

**Phone**
For calls within the 5 boroughs
311
For calls outside the 5 boroughs
(212) 639-9675

**Address**
Borough Hall Building
10 Richmond Terrace, Room 311,
Staten Island, NY 10301

# Officiant

## MANHATTAN ....................................................................................

### A New York City Wedding by Reverend Will

Traditional, Spiritual, Civil, Commitment, Interfaith, New Age, Same Sex.

Non-denominational, Buddhist, Christian, Hindu, Protestant, Roman Catholic, Islamic.

**Website**
revwill.com

**Contact**
Reverend Dr. C. William Mercer

**Email**
Contact through website

**Phone**
(646) 753-2959

**Address**
155 E. 105th Street,
Suite 2B,
New York, NY 10029

### Art of the Ceremony

Civil Union, Interfaith, Non-religious, Single Religion, Same Sex.

Agnostic, Buddhist, Hindu, Christian (non-denominational), Islam, Jewish, Muslim, Taoist.

**Website**
artoftheceremony.com

**Contact**
Reverend Peluso

**Email**
artoftheceremony@yahoo.com or artoftheceremony@aol.com

**Phone**
(212) 724-4880

**Address**
West 86 Street & Central Park West,
New York, NY 10024

### Common Ground Ceremonies

Civil Union, Commitment Ceremonies, Interfaith, New Age, Non-religious, Single Religion, Same Sex, Vow Renewals.

Buddhist, Catholic, Earth-Based, Episcopalian, Evangelical, Hindu, Islam, Jainism, Jewish, Lutheran, Methodist, No Denomination, Pagan, Presbyterian, Quaker, Shinto, Sikhism, Taoist, Unitarian.

**Website**
commongroundceremonies.com

**Contact**
Reverend Samora Smith

**Email**
rev.samora@gmail.com

**Phone**
(646) 709-2090

**Address**
711 E. 11th Street, New York, NY 10009

### Jester of the Peace

Civil Union, Interfaith, Non-religious, Single Religion, Rehearsal, Commitment Ceremonies, New Age, Vow Renewal.

Agnostic, Anglican, Baha'i Faith, Baptist, Buddhist, Catholic, Earth-Based, Episcopalian, Evangelical, Hindu, Islam, Jainism, Jewish, Lutheran, Methodist, Mormon, No Denomination, Orthodox Christian, Pagan, Presbyterian, Quaker, Shinto, Sikhism, Taoist, Unitarian.

**Website**
jesterofthepeace.com

**Contact**
Wedding Officiant: Barbara Ann Michael

**Email**
barbara@jesterofthepeace.com

**Phone**
(646) 648-0128

**Address**
New York, NY

## Lynn Gladstone

Traditional and Non-traditional, Same Sex, Later Marriages, Commitment Ceremonies, Elopements, Vow Renewals, New Age.

Buddhist, Catholic, Christian, Hindu, Jewish, Muslim, Non-Denominational/Secular.

**Website**
lynngladstone.com

**Contact**
Reverend Lynn Gladstone

**Email**
lynn@lynngladstone.com

**Phone**
(914) 552-5567

**Address**
New York, NY

## Phillips Ceremonies

Civil Marriages, Commitment Ceremonies, Interfaith, New Age, Premarital Counseling.

Buddhist, Jewish, Non-Denominational/Secular.

**Website**
phillipsceremonies.com

**Contact**
NYC Wedding Officiant, Minister & Celebrant
Adam Phillips

**Email**
adam@phillipsceremonies.com

**Phone**
(917) 670-9293

**Address**
532 W. 111th Street, New York, NY 10025

## Reverend Annie Lawrence

Civil Marriages, Commitment Ceremonies, Interfaith, New Age, Same Sex, Civil Unions, Non-religious, Single Religion, Vow Renewal, Rehearsal.

Buddhist, Catholic, Christian, Jewish, Muslim, Non-Denominational/Secular.

**Website**
revannielawrence.com

**Contact**
Ordained Interfaith Minister & Licensed Wedding Officiant
Reverend Annie Lawrence

**Email**
revannielawrence@gmail.com

**Phone**
(917) 620-6307

**Address**
New York, NY

## Reverend Lawrence Grecco, Buddhist Monk

Interfaith, Non-religious, Single Religion, Same Sex.

Agnostic, Anglican, Baha'i Faith, Baptist, Buddhist, Catholic, Episcopalian, Evangelical, Hindu, Islam, Jainism, Jewish, Lutheran, Methodist, Mormon, No Denomination, Orthodox Christian, Presbyterian, Quaker, Shinto, Sikhism, Taoist.

**Website**
revgrecco.com

**Contact**
Zen Buddhist Monk & Wedding Officiant
Reverend Lawrence Grecco

**Email**
revgrecco@gmail.com

**Phone**
(212) 989-3456

**Address**
New York, NY

## Reverend Louis Olivieri

Civil Union, Interfaith, Non-religious, Commitment Ceremonies, Same Sex, LGBT.

Agnostic, Anglican, Baptist, Buddhist, Catholic, Episcopalian, Evangelical, Hindu, Jewish, Lutheran, Methodist, Mormon, No Denomination, Orthodox Christian, Presbyterian, Quaker, Shinto, Sikhism, Taoist.

**Website**
revlouisolivieri.com

**Contact**
Reverend Louis Olivieri

**Email**
revlouisolivieri@aol.com

**Phone**
(917) 656-0929

## Reverend Sandra Bargman

Civil Union, Commitment Ceremonies, Interfaith, New Age, Elopements, Vow Renewals, Costume and Holiday Weddings, Same Sex.

Christian, Non-Denominational/Secular, all spiritual beliefs and practices.

**Website**
revsandrabargman.com

**Contact**
Ordained Interfaith Minister, Spiritual Counselor & Wedding Officiant Reverend Sandra Bargman

**Email**
info@revsandrabargman.com

**Phone**
(917) 627-9804

**Address**
New York, NY

## Spirited Weddings with Deborah Roth

Civil Union, Interfaith, New Age, Non-denominational, Non religious, Rehearsal, Vow Renewal.

Agnostic, Anglican, Baptist, Buddhist, Catholic, Earth-Based, Episcopalian, Hindu, Islam, Jewish, Lutheran, Methodist, No Denomination, Pagan, Presbyterian, Quaker, Shinto, Unitarian.

**Website**
spiritedliving.com

**Contact**
Reverend Deborah Roth

**Email**
deborah@spiritedliving.com

**Phone**
(212) 665-9660

**Address**
270 Riverside Drive, Suite 1C, New York, NY 10025

## Tulis McCall - Wedding Celebrant

Civil Union, Interfaith, Non-religious, Single Religion, Same Sex.

Agnostic, Anglican, Baha'i Faith, Baptist, Buddhist, Catholic, Earth-Based, Episcopalian, Evangelical, Hindu, Islam, Jainism, Jewish, Lutheran, Methodist, Mormon, No Denomination, Orthodox Christian, Pagan, Presbyterian, Quaker, Shinto, Sikhism, Taoist, Unitarian.

**Website**
weddingsbytulis.com or newyorkweddingofficiant.com

**Contact**
Wedding Officiant & Interfaith Minister Tulis McCall

**Email**
info@newyorkweddingofficiant.com

**Phone**
(917) 318-8943

**Address**
1 W. 57th Street, New York, NY 10019

# BROOKLYN......................

## Brooklyn Society For Ethical Culture
Interfaith, Secular, Same Sex.

Provides an officiate, and requires at least two meetings to plan a ceremony.

**Website**
http://www.bsec.org/#!about-us/c1se

**Contact**
Damal Edmond

**Email**
bsecdirector@yahoo.com

**Phone**
(718) 768-2972

**Address**
53 Prospect Park West,
Brooklyn, NY 11215

# WESTCHESTER....................

## Rabbi Andrea Frank
Civil Union, Interfaith Ceremonies, Non-religious, Single Religion, Vow Renewal, Spiritual Weddings, Elopement Ceremonies, Same-sex, LGBT.

Jewish

**Website**
jewish-wedding-rabbi.com

**Contact**
Ordained Reform Rabbi
Rabbi Andrea Frank

**Phone**
(888) 214-3821

**Address**
Westchester County, NY

# QUEENS.................................

## Nautical Wedding Bells (Specialty: weddings at sea)
Civil Union, Interfaith, Non-religious, Single Religion, Vow Renewal.

Agnostic, Baha'i Faith, Buddhist, Christian (no denomination), Anglican, Baptist, Catholic, Episcopalian, Lutheran, Methodist, Mormon, Orthodox Christian, Presbyterian, Quaker, Evangelical, Hindu, Islam, Jainism, Jewish, Muslim, Shinto, Sikhism, Taoist.

**Website**
nauticalweddingbells.com

**Contact**
Captain Arnold, Interfaith Chaplain

**Email**
captarnold@gmail.com

**Phone**
(516) 413-4555 or (718) 767-6242

**Address**
18-05 215th Street, Bayside, NY 11360

# NOTES

# NOTES

# NOTES

# NOTES

# NOTES

# NOTES

# NOTES

# NOTES

# NOTES

# NOTES

www.ingramcontent.com/pod-product-compliance
Lightning Source LLC
Chambersburg PA
CBHW041221270326
41932CB00006B/44